Playing with the Cards That You've Been Dealt

Learning How to Live with What You've Already Been Given

Jazmiera Janay

ACKNOWLEDGEMENTS

To my Mother- *Mom you are amazing. You have driven me to be the best mother, daughter, and friend that I could possibly be. Without your loving support and encouragement I'm sure I wouldn't have ever made it this far. We bump heads all of the time but that's just us, I love you unconditionally even if I may not say it much. Thank you for keeping up with Pop Pop as I tried my best to get this done. Thank you for EVERYTHING.*

To My Best Friends- *Natalie and Brittany I can never repay either of you for all that you've done for both my son and I. Both of you came into my life right on time and I must honestly say it is amazing how you both make yourselves available to always be there for me whenever I need you. Natalie, I thank you for always being around when I needed someone to keep Pop occupied while I got some things done. Brittany, I thank you for pushing me to be my best every time I'd speak about giving up. I love you both and truly appreciate you. When I get rich, you both can have whatever you want.*

To My Prayer Sister- *Latisha, you have been the angel in disguise that has drawn me closer to the Lord. You keep me level headed and I'm not sure how you manage to always be around when you've got so much going on yourself, but you are always here and I appreciate it. Continue to be strong because I need you in my life. I know that we will both be okay and I pray that you stay in my life forever because I need you to help me get through it all. I love you.*

DEDICATION

This book is dedicated to my son, Na'zier Jr.
You are the missing piece to the puzzle of my life and when I get the
chance to make us wealthy, it'll all be for you.
Thank you for being mommy's everyday motivation and thank you for
always keeping me going.
You may not be able to read this now, but someday I hope you get the
chance to see this.
You saved my life.
I love you so much, and thank you.

Table of Contents

Introduction:

Hey all! For those who may not know me personally, my name is Jazmiera but you can just call me Jazz (yes that used to be my Instagram tag). Over the course of the last month or so I made the decision to start a blogging website that is used to encourage and to empower other young mothers to make it through each day the same way that I manage to make it through mine. Throughout the website I inserted blogs and stories that could help mothers to view things from a different perspective. After making this decision and launching my site, it was then that my blogs began to touch the hearts of more than just the young moms.

I started getting feedback from women, men, and young adults nationwide all the way down to Europe; who had all be influenced by my writing and my stories. It amazed me to see how so many people had become in tuned with what it was that I was writing and to see that they enjoyed it so much to the point where they even decided to reach out to me.

After talking with all of the viewers, I had decided that I wanted to turn all of my stories and experiences into a life changing novel.

"Playing with the Cards that You've Been Dealt" came to mind because a card game is filled with options and instructions that are anonymous to you at the beginning of the game. When your cards are drawn to you, you have no idea what they may be because they are faced down; just like you how you never know what's coming your way in life.

I have taken the card game analogy and compared it to the way life works as far as using and managing what it is that you've already been given.

I hope you all can enjoy this read and I also hope that you gain something out of it as I try and help each and every one of you to GROW through what it is that you're GOING through. Best of luck to you all in your game of life,

-XOXO JAZZ

Chapter 1: Life is a Game

When we are first born into this world, our gift has already been giving to us. Sometimes it may seem as if we were just put on this earth to serve and to survive but really there's a purpose behind why each and every one of us are here.

The game of life can be intimidating once you start your journey into adulthood but it is important that we never allow failure to slow us down. Challenges are put into our lives in order for us to be able to stay strong and to test our capabilities. Now I know it may seem as if every day is a challenge and that there aren't many good days; but that's just a part of the game. When you fail to realize that you are the one who is in control of what happens in your life, then there's no way you can change your viewpoint and perspective about different aspects in the world. We classify the idea of living as hard compared to no longer being alive because, when you're no longer alive there's nothing left for you to be responsible for.

Reread that line again, and let it sink in.

I'm here to let you know that life can be so much better and you can be the driver behind the greatness that can come out of your day to day living.

Sometimes we tend to make decisions based off of our wants instead of our needs and that causes stressors to occur. When there is something that is given to you, take it and see where the opportunity leads you.

If you're unhappy, then let it go.

Realistically, no one can just let that nine to five job go because there are responsibilities such as your bills at home and children that need to eat. But, what's a life if it is built off of settling and how can that benefit you besides financial help?

Find your niche in life and grow from there by never settling for less then what it is that you want out of this game.

When you think about how you envision your life to actually be, you have to focus on what it is that you have in your possession now in order to start working with it.

Just like when playing a card game; you're given cards that are flipped upside down so that you never know what you have until you flip them over. Once you flip those cards over then your weapons are revealed and you must figure out how to use them to your benefit. Although you may not be satisfied with the cards that have been dealt, you have to begin the game and use your other resources in the middle of the deck of cards to continue on.

Take the necessities that you've been given in life and make something out of them. Do not let your mind be convicted of the fact that you do not have enough right now.

Not enough money. Not enough friends. Not enough time.

Living without being satisfied is the first step of failing at this game.

If you continue to complain and to allow the amount of what you've been given to stop you from living then that's a red flag. You must realize how important your life is to you, and use what you have been given to make it the best.

A lot of us use the phrase "not enough" often and never do anything about that "not enough" situation.

If you feel as if you do not have enough income, then start looking for another job or something to do on the side.

If you're all out of friends and feel alone, then start networking and meeting new people.

You see?

Everything that we complain about can be changed as long as we make time to see results from it.

Nothing in life is handed to you and I'm sure most of you are aware of this.

Everything that you have in your possession required you to do something first in order to receive it. The job that you have, you had to go on an interview to get it. The friends that you have now, you had to make conversation with them first in order to even give them the title of being a friend.

Continue to use what you have been given to get what it is that you want.

We were given a body to use for purposes such as working, and getting around.

We were given a name to tell us apart from everyone else, so why not use it as a brand?

We were given a mind to help us with figuring out things in life, so why not use it to figure out where it is that you need to be exactly?

As people, we spend so much time reflecting on the worse scenarios that we've been through and fail to look at the small things that have come our way. We fail to appreciate the fact that we've been given another set of twenty four hours to try again at whatever it was that we failed at yesterday. We never accept the fact that the hand that we were given could be so much worse.

I now work downtown in Baltimore, Maryland and when I say the individuals out here have helped me to appreciate my life so much more, they truly have. Even those that may not be homeless have had an impact on my viewpoint of life. Their homes aren't taken care of like the homes in my development, their stores aren't as up to date as our stores are, and the streets that they are expected to live on are far from even being clean. It is heartbreaking to know that people are living like this, but it also can tear you apart to know that this could've been your hand of cards that you were dealt when the game first started. Appreciate what it is that you have, and teach your children to appreciate it too. You can never be happy in life if you're never satisfied with what you have to live with. Yes money is needed for everything and it may feel like you can never have enough; but think about how far you've come.

For a moment just reflect back on all of the times when you thought that you wouldn't be able to manage or to get something done because you felt like there was nothing left. As you think about those times, realize that you're still here and you still have that car or that house now even though you thought that there was no way it could be paid for. Begin to realize that you always make a way out of no way and regardless of how stressful something may seem in that moment; always remember that it will get better.

I personally know that I am not happy with the way things are going in my life right now. It seems as if every day is a day that I must push and fight through in order to get to the end because I am not satisfied with how it is going.

I feel as if I am one of those who settles for whatever comes my way when I need it the most; just like settling for jobs because you need money and you need it right away; so sign me up for whatever.

One time Y'all, I found myself on indeed applying for jobs that would require me to move bulldozers and to pick up packages that were 90 pounds and up.

Yeah, can you say desperate? I'm only 105 pounds myself. Try again Jazz.

This is why I am letting you all know that I do not want you to feel the way that I feel, I need you all to be better than me.

The point behind me teaching you the lesson of the game is to stop you from going through what it is that I am going through. My goal is to help you all realize the things that I wish I would've known before making some of the decisions in my life. Although most of my readers may be older than me, it is true that I can still teach some of you a lesson about rethinking the way that you've been playing your cards.

The main point of playing is to start with whatever you have and to work your way around turning it all into something that you really want.

If whatever you want requires more money, then begin by saving the smallest amount even though we all tend to believe that saving is impossible.

If whatever you want requires more time, then talk to your boss about your schedule and give yourself more time in your day. Or if that will not work, then every minute you spend on social media should go towards a minute of time that you invest in yourself.

Excuses are what gets in the way of most of our success stories.

We all find a way to stray away from something because we're afraid of failure and afraid of investing in ourselves. If you are a person who spends that last three dollars on a scratch off to see if you can make a come up, you're the same person that can hold on to that three dollars and add a few more to it in order to start something great.

"Invest in yourself before you invest in the riches' wealth"-Jazz.

I created this quote myself to remind everyone about how much we invest in the latest inventions before we even put money aside for ourselves.

When people complain to me about how broke they are and how they never have money I always ask them this: "What was the last item that you purchased?" Usually it's food from a high dollar restaurant, the latest technology, the newest car, or the newest pair of shoes. When some makes the decision to spend money irresponsibly it eventually becomes a repeated habit. You may see it occur once or twice every two weeks because that's when they usually tend to receive a paycheck. Yes it is important to purchase things that you enjoy so that you can enjoy your life; but imagine how much more you would enjoy it if you kept your money to yourself and started investing in something you love?

I'm an adult now so I understand that money is taken away from you as soon as you make it, but think about how you're playing with those cards first.

In order to change, you have to look at where your problems are stemming from and decide to do something about it.

Therefore, look at all of the transactions that are coming out of your account. If there are any subscriptions that are not needed then get rid of them. Begin by eliminating anything that can slow you down or stop you from beginning your new game. Focus on the bad first and then see if you notice a difference. Again, being an adult now helps me to understand that this life is not easy but I also know that the problems we have were created by no one except ourselves.

Along the lines of this book there are a lot of segments that'll make you think twice about some of the decisions and habits that you've created or have been making. I hope to enter a different part of your mind and to help you to use the reference of a card game to help you better understand the way that life goes.

Each chapter will be a reference to either a card that is in a deck or a reference on instructions of how to play the game. The references will be life tips and pointers that can help you to see the way that you're living from a different perspective.

This is the end of chapter one, and I hope you all are ready to play as we begin with the instructions in chapter two.

Chapter 2: Instructions on Positivity

In life there are many obstacles out there that will try and stop us from being great, but it is our job to continue in the game until we win. Although every time you lose in a game it requires you to then start all over, that's okay because you never know what you're going to get the next time around. Whenever we get discouraged or afraid of what can happen next, sometimes we begin to fall off and give up. During this phase we tend to drop whatever it is that we were working on and end up moving backwards instead of forward. Like the saying says, "Move 8 steps forward then 10 steps back."

Did you know that you're in control of your reaction to those 8 and then 10 steps? Some of us tend to forget that life is what we make it so we shut down and shut out any possibilities of getting back up and taking another 8 steps forward. When life tries to challenge you and deals you a hand of cards that aren't exactly what you expected, you still have to play. If you were to say "I don't think I can play" or "I'm not sure what to do with this hand", then that means you gave up and automatically let your opponent win.

The instructions to getting through all of this are as follows:

Start by writing out the main goal that you have in your mind.

Use this goal, and take what you have been given in life to decide what it is that you must do first in order to accomplish the goal properly.

One by one, knockout those options until you're left with your goal mastered and completed.

Talk about your results, and be proud of your last draw that got you to the end of the game as the winner.

STEP 1: Writing Out Your Goal

When writing out your goal, this step is just like agreeing to play in the game. After deciding to play, you then look at your options for accomplishing your goal just like picking up those first 5 to 8 cards that had been drawn out to you in order to play in the game. Everyone wants to win in life but no one ever knows where to start or how to begin. Although you may have no idea what that hand of cards consist of, you have to take what you're given and make the smartest moves for the best results.

By writing out your goals it increases your envision of what your results are going to be. Some people tend to create vision boards that they place somewhere for them to be able to see it every day. On that vision board are images of the goals that people are ready to focus on accomplishing and there are also steps and words that stand out to them which remind them about what it is that they must do.

Start here.

Start with your vision board and then move forward from there. It doesn't have to be as fancy as others because you're your own person but, be sure to make it something that satisfies your needs and wants. Use this time of creation and use it as your inspiration in order to GO, giving yourself the greenlight on what it is that you really want in life. One thing that can be hard about this part is actually beginning the steps it takes to reach the goals that you have written down. With everything that's happening in this world it tends to be very hard to stay focused and to do what's actually needed of you to do in order to get to where it is that you may want to be. If you can write these goals out on paper then guess what? This means that you've already started on the right path in this game of life. You've taken the first step of reading the instructions on how to play.

Never get discouraged after you write those goals down by thinking, "This is insane I'm way out of my league with this one." No one is ever out of their league when it comes to what they're capable of doing so JUST DO IT! I challenge you all today to take the time and to actually follow instruction number one; which is to write out your goal and what you'll being using to play while on your journey to creating your future. Before I make my next statement let me just say, I have an infinite amount of viewers reading this today (at least I hope) but I'd like to speak to those who may be thinking "Jazz is crazy, I am too old to start over in this game of life."

NO MATTER HOW OLD YOU MAY BE, IF YOU ARE STILL WLAKING THIS EARTH YOU CAN DO THE UNTHINKABLE.

A lot of people tend to spend time thinking about all of the reasons as to why they CANNOT accomplish their goals list instead of using their resources and figuring out HOW to accomplish their goals. Age means nothing to someone when you believe and have faith in yourself. If you want to be the same size that you were when you were 22 and you're now 40, THEN GO FOR IT. If you want to change that townhouse into a penthouse, THEN GO FOR IT!

If you've never used the benefit of starting that 401k plan with your job but you really wanted to, THEN GO FOR IT!

Never say never guys; the sky is the limit and if you know that you can keep going or that you have the potential to create something new then turn those thoughts into a reality and begin the process towards the end of your list of goals. After you have chosen to be dealt a hand of cards (entering the game with your 5 to 8 options), you have to be mindful of the fact that your cards are flipped over until you pick them up, but once you pick up those cards and see what you have been given, it's go time and we must make the best of what it is that we already have because we are NOT backing down and allowing our opponent to win.

STEP 2: Use Your Resources

From experience and also after watching my grandmother and family members play the card game of Tonk when I was a little girl, the first thing my grandma always taught me how to do was how to rearrange those cards in order as to how you may want to throw them down.

So with the things that you have been given in life, place them in order as to how they can benefit you and your goal for the remainder of this game. If you have a car, then that means you have transportation to get to wherever you may need to go when it is needed to contribute to your goals. If you have a job, you have a source of income that you may or may not be able to put aside to help you but, there is always the slightest chance that any dollar or dime can add up and be useful.

With that being said, grab yourself a piggy bank and stop leaving that penny, nickel, or dime on the ground when you're walking out from the store because you'll be needing those to contribute to your goal from now on.

If you have friends, family, or any loved ones around, let them know that you're about to take off and that you need them to be ready to support you all the way. I personally have my team of four that get a text message from me every day based off of what it is that may be happening in my life right now. The first one is my prayer sister, another is my best friend that keeps it real (she hurts my feelings but the truth is always necessary), another is my best friend who never lets me give up, and the last one is my mother. I would never be able to live without these women and that's just real. Use those around you that can be there for you without them feeling threatened by your success.

Take a step back, and read that again.

If you're reading this part of the book and saying "Yeah right, no one wants to see me win around here" then HOUSTON WE HAVE A PROBLEM! It's now time for you to get yourself a new set of friends that can become family, a prayer group that can become your warriors, and a whole other host of individuals that can push you to be the very best that you can be. Like I said I only have four, and two of them became a part of my team not even a year ago.

Let me be real with you for a moment; the people you may have started with can or cannot be the people that you end with. Never see this as an upsetting situation, see it as a blessing because someone took those individuals out of your life for a reason. They may have been your "Day Ones" but when you're about to take off and make it to the top, if they're not interested in seeing you win trust me they'll become "The End of the Weeks" quickly and vanish like that person ready to get out of work for the weekend. It's time that you start networking by meeting new people and seeing new faces because you're going to need a team regardless, trust me. This village card is like an Ace, without that village behind you there's no telling if you'll ever make it. You cannot do this alone and that's just a fact; you need a team of your top 4's.

STEP 3: Play until the End

As the game continues on, you're going to continue to throw your cards out or you may choose to draw more cards in order to stay in the game. Just like the game, you'll have to make the same decision in life as well. If your heart says it's time to let that hurt go from that last relationship because it's slowing you down; LET IT GO. If your mind is saying "I can't afford this new car anymore I've got to find something cheaper" then take that Mercedes back and stop trying to keep up with the Jones'. You aren't where you're supposed to be in life right now so who cares about what's happening around you. Those people that you're trying to keep up with, they've already made it. Or to say the least, they don't mind pulling up to their mama's house in a 2018 Tessler because they're content with that. You want more, so screw them and their Tessler and go get you the latest Honda Accord that probably looks similar to a Tessler now a days anyway.

Continue to drop the things that are not meant for you, and pick up those new cards that could help you empty out that hand faster. Watch as your opponent continues to try and beat you to the end as they throw out cards to try and slow you down. Life throws out challenges almost every day that can make you feel as if there's no point of even going any further. Envision this scenario for a second. You're playing a game of UNO and it's down to the last two players, you and your opponent.

Your opponent drops that last card before the end and looks up to you grinning and says "UNO". Now there you are looking silly with 8 cards in your hand giving your opponent a sense of security because that line of 8 cards in your hand will be stuck there until the end. But, you've got a surprise for them. Every last card in your hand is the color blue plus a draw 4. You've got two BLUE Draw 2's (which CAN go on top of each other if you want them to), you've got two BLUE Skips, 2 BLUE reverses and one card that's a BLUE number two.

Can you say game over?

YOU WIN!!

Your opponent is left devastated but at the end of the day, you've won this game of life! Again, there's no telling what cards may come your way but as long as you're playing it smart; who cares about what other people may feel or think. The game has now come to an end and the goal that you were trying to achieve has become reality; you won and now you're going to continue to win because that is something that your opponent cannot take away from you even if they say "There's no way I lost, we've got to play this again." It's too late, you're already the winner and there's no telling what you'll be capable of when they draw out that next set of cards to you. You see, all you had to do was follow the instructions on how to play the game and in return for following those instructions you were giving the opportunity to actually feel what it's like to win. Now back to the topic at hand which is the game of positivity.

Whenever you choose to grow through the game of life you have to put on your armor and get ready to face the toughest trials and tribulations that were ever created. Yes it feels good to do something right in life but let me just tell you something; I've had more days when I was ready to give up then I did spending time celebrating my success. Nothing worth having comes as easy as they say so therefore, you must always prepare for the worse even when things seem to be going just after nothing felt right for the longest time. The trial and error period of spending time doing what it is that you have to do can always be the hardest. When I first decided to become a blogger and writer I had no idea why I felt this urge, but I knew that I needed to do some research because I had never did neither one of those things in my life before. I used both of my main resources (Google and Pinterest) to find the latest "How to's" and "What to look out for's". Again, I went into this business blindsided so there was no way I could just make this happen on my own. I had to put in the time and begin investing in myself even if the reviews said that a site didn't work for one person but it worked for another; sometimes I'd take that risk or two. This gets us back to the saying "you never know what you're going to get"; just always remember that it is better to say that you've tried then to say that you never even attempted.

SO my friend, get ready to face the things that work for you and the things that could just make your situation harder and more challenging. Never doubt the fact of the matter which is that you can teach yourself how to do anything.

As I read the articles from Pinterest and Google, a lot of writers referred me to links that would charge me to do things that I HONESTLY DID ON MY OWN! From coming up with my own templates for my site, creating my own book cover, and doing a host of other things, I've probably saved over hundreds of dollars that would've just been a waste. Now don't get me wrong, I have invested in myself time and time again spending my last to make it to this day but it was WORTH IT! Everything that I had to take out has now been invested back into me thanks to you all (again, a village). If you know me personally, you'd know that I'm never without a smile in public. Although I tend to wear my heart on my sleeve and it's easy to tell when something's gone wrong; I never let it depict my work ethnic or change the way that I move. There's been time and time again where I've failed to realize that something from my life was missing in the beginning. I had always thought a problem needed a reaction and that a blessing needed a praise. Whenever something went wrong, I'd get angry and cause a whole fit over the situation. While I'm having my tantrum, I failed to realize that no one was hurting in that moment but me. You guys should have seen me during this phase in life; punching walls, driving recklessly, anything you name I probably have done it out of anger. It took me a few years to realize that I was the only one hurting from my actions and in an instant I changed. It was like it had happened over night or something.

I didn't want to feel the way that I felt anymore; it was a burden and a blinder to where I was trying to go in life. BTW, this just happened for me only about a week ago. Check out my blog "Commuting Disturbance: Learning How to Change a Life Challenge into a Life Lesson". In this blog you'll learn about how I turned this long and dreading commute that I have at the moment into something positive because guess what? I DON'T HAVE A CHOICE! In order to continue to invest in myself and to let go of this 9-5, I must first take this commute to my job and continue to grow my income. The goal is to always see the good in everything that seems like a disturbance. If you walk around mad at the world because your car isn't the latest; then that's on you. If you decide to walk around mad at the world because your boyfriend didn't take you to red lobster and instead he took you to Wendy's because you said "I don't know" when asked; then that's on YOU!

But my goal here is to convince you all to try something different for once. I need you all to push the gas on those older model vehicles right down the highway towards whatever place that can benefit your goals. Ladies, I need you to accept wherever you end up eating at and grab something to eat which in your mind resembles that lobster tail or steak (besides you said "I don't know anyway").

MAKE THE BEST OUT OF EVERYTHING IN LIFE!

Stop letting the little things interrupt your success when there are way bigger problems and wind tides headed your way. There are things that are about to blow your mind, but you must be prepared for them by standing strong with a positive attitude and a mind that's ready to fight back. Stop making excuses for your behavior as far as your attitude and begin to change instantly, just like I did. Now who's to say that I've perfected or mastered this positive thing? Not me. But on the other hand, I do know some people that can testify to my growth in this process and that's my village. They are witnesses to the outcome of my changes, and now look at me writing a book and stuff. *GO JAZZ, GO JAZZ* Change is great my friends and it can do something for you that it has never done before. Take a minute and look back on all that you have accomplished so far; I mean all the way back to the first time that you ever tied your shoes and your mama teared up at it! That right there seems like something small, but from now on every time you bend down to tie those shoes be proud of it because one day long ago you didn't know how to tie them at all. Remember all of the feelings that you've felt every time you accomplished something in life and allow that feeling to hit you right in this moment. Did you just feel that? How your heart feels all warm, and how your lips decided to crack a quick smile?

If not, then sorry that was only me.

If you DID feel it, I want you to begin to feel that feeling every time you knock a step off of your list of options. For each option there may be different steps that you must take, but never be afraid to take it one at a time. Trying to accomplish everything at once can be very overwhelming and can drift us back into that negative attitude which we don't want to do. Take EACH step and break it down into their own new set of steps. For a moment I'm taking us back to my grandma sitting at that table rearranging her cards. I need you to put everything in order as to how you can properly manage and win at life. Whatever you have been given in life, use it but use it in a proper manner. Be smart with those cards (moves) that you're about to make.

"Never let the fear of striking out keep you from playing the game"-Cinderella Story.

I used this quote as a reference in my graduation speech last month to let my classmates know that after that day, life was about to pick up for us all. I say this to tell you all to never be afraid of putting down a card because you're afraid of what can happen next. It could've been frightening earlier if you didn't know how to play UNO and you would've threw out that BLUE 2 card instead of throwing out that draw 4 first because you know why? Your opponent could've had a BLUE 3, and the game would've been finished for you. But instead, you rearranged those cards in your hand and started throwing them out while also making it to the end with the winner's title. I hope you guys are keeping up with me at this point because things are about to drift in a different direction as I introduce you to the power of the mind.

The mind has a way of playing a game itself even when we're trying to play a different game of our own. Sometimes you'll hesitate and get torn between following your heart and doing what your mind is telling you to do. This can become very frustrating for us and can cause us to never make any of our next moves because we're afraid of the outcome. It is time that you start to understand your mind and get to know both yourself and the way that you tend to think. If you never get to know yourself, then how will you know what it is that you'd like to do and how far you'd be willing to go? Some people find studying the mind to be weird but I must say I disagree. I spent my best years of high school with Mr. Biggs while trying to see things from his perspective and then I went on to college thinking that by this time now I'd be graduating with my bachelors in psychology.

LOL jokes on me.

I ended up graduating this year from a medical assistant program through Towson University that landed me a job in the "Behavioral Medicine Research Lab" as a medical technician. MIND BLOWING! Did you guys catch that? Although I graduated from a medical assistant program, that's not the job that I ended up with. Somehow my life still linked me back to psychology and now I work with patients to see how their bodies and minds react to certain medications and placebos. Funny isn't it?

How I began to feel as if the psych field was no longer for me, then all of a sudden I got swooped right back in by this thing called LIFE. There is a place that was destined for me, a dream and a goal that I always wanted to reach and that was just to be RICH. It doesn't matter how I get there, as long as I get there is my goal. Being that I love the mind and psychology (the study of the mind) so much, it still follows me wherever I go because that is where my energy shifts towards. I love people, I love the idea behind figuring out why we do the things that we do and I hope to put an impact on a lot of people's hearts before my time comes to an end. Now here we are again, trying to see what's next for me in life because I still haven't reached my goal of making an impact on people's lives. But, here I am sitting in front of a computer screen typing my first book ever to MAKE AN IMPACT ON PEOPLE'S LIVES!

Man, life has a funny way of working something out and I hope that you all are reading this and taking it all in because my story can also become your story. Even when we think that something may not be meant for us because we threw away a card in relations to what it is that we want to do; always remember that there may be a card in that deck that can bring you right back to where it all started in the first place. This is why I need you all to understand the steps and instructions of the game because the way to play is to watch yourself make it to the end and have your name written on the winner's seat.

Ever use your GPS and make a wrong turn, then your screen says "rerouting" and you're afraid that you're going to go the wrong way again? Well, let me tell you a quick story. Today on my way to work I was driving and so zoned out on the fact that I was about to be launching a book in three weeks that could possibly make me rich; I made a wrong turn. GPS starts redirecting me and I get nervous because I knew that the new route had nothing but extensive traffic. I didn't grow angry (because remember I'm working on this attitude thing) I just followed along and snapped back into being on the road. As I'm driving, signs on the highway begin to look familiar to me. Little did I know, I ended up right back on the route that I take to work every day and somehow I no longer needed the GPS because I knew where I was going from there.

You see how that worked?

That story pertains to life because sometimes we may make the wrong decision but at the end of the day what's meant for us will always be for us and we will somehow find our way again. It may feel like the roads to the end are never ending and that you'll never see the last step of the game but trust me your time is coming.

STEP 4: Celebrate Your Results

As you were reading along you probably thought "Jazz, you've skipped step 4." Or maybe you were so in tuned to the reading that you didn't even notice. But, Jazz had a plan and now here we are at step four.

This is the last step of the game but it is also the BEST instruction of the game. It is time for you to celebrate, to rejoice for all that you've been through and to make noise about what it is that you've done. There is never a time where you accomplish something and you tend to not celebrate it (unless you're just an "it is what it is" kind of person), we always want to feel good about what it is that we've done. So take the time after you've completed all of your goals and give yourself a pat on the back for a job well done. It wasn't easy to get there I'm sure and you didn't do it for nothing. We all have a reason behind why we do the things that we do so therefore feel good my friend because you've won at the game of life for another time.

Do something nice for yourself once you make it. Refer back to your village and remember who was there throughout the toughest times and return the favor by giving your top 5's something that they've always wanted. In return of your success, put a smile on other people's faces and continue to live your now new best life. Never feel as if you can't celebrate your greatness when you deserve to. I've noticed that in my generation, a lot of people tend to distract you and make you feel as if celebrating your success is stupid because it's what you're supposed to be doing but let them know that this was NOT easy and that it was NOT handed to you.

SHOUT TO THE SKIES FOR ALL THAT YOU'VE ACCOMPLISHED AND NEVER LET ANYONE STEAL YOUR JOY OF FINALLY MAKING IT.

Now reversing back again like an UNO card, I'd like to talk about the road of life. The road seems very long when you're looking forward to something but have you ever noticed how fast the time goes by? The worst thing you can do to yourself is watch as time travels on. Counting the days, the minutes, and the hours is the least bit of help for you because then your mind begins to grow anxious. Sometimes I think it's fair to say that most of us never realize that we have control over our own minds. When there are things that seem to be out of whack, the mind automatically jumps in to panic mode and then we begin to worry along with the feeling of fear that something can go wrong. JUST THAT FAST we've lost the control of our mind because everything happened so quickly.

It is important that we begin to drive our minds in the right direction being that there's a better chance for us to be successful if we were able to choose the way that we think. Begin by looking at things from a different perspective. Imagine yourself turning every bad situation into something good and how much of a difference it can make on your mind and soul. It can release any toxins that make it harder to be you and it can help you to remember that not every challenge is a struggle. At times the challenges we face can be beneficial to us because they can teach us a lesson that may be harder to learn from anyone else. Looking at life from a positive mind state helps you to see the good in everything that you do.

Ah, lightbulb.

Flaws are the biggest factor in the underlining vision of our minds. I know for me, it isn't a secret that I can point out every single flaw that I have. I tend to focus more so on my flaws then I do on my strengths because well, that's a part of my depression. No matter how many times I try and see the good in myself, the darkness that hides behind my mind seems to always strike again. Please stop yourselves from being like me and work on finding the good within in yourself. Never stop from being the best that you can be and always remember that you're capable of anything. With this mindset, you'll be willing to try and go for anything that comes your way just like the risks that you must take to get this game started.

Chapter 3: Playing with an ACE

I n chapter two I referenced the ace card to your village, which is the most important part of being successful. Over the last three weeks I have decided to come up with this blogging website as a hobby and career that has shifted my attention and goals into a different direction. Although it seems to be impossible for someone to just do it over night, here I am making it happen and succeeding within a matter of a few weeks. It has been very easy to create everything that is needed for what I want to do, but the hardest part of it all has been getting the support and publicity that I need in order for me to be successful.

Everyone started off by saying that I had their full support, but as soon as I continued to share my content and show off the success behind it, I began to lose followers on Facebook and my likes and comments begun to decrease. Sometimes people may say that they support you time and time again, but as soon as you begin to take off and grow in your field of success it's as if they've vanished off of the earth. The people that begin to vanish are the ones that are intimidated by your success and afraid that you'll make it before they do.

These are the individuals that you must look out for. I know me posting my blogs every 3-4 hours can be repetitive and annoying but its good content; and the content cannot be seen unless it is shared and viewed. It hurts sometimes to know that people will unfollow you because they're tired of seeing you try your best to achieve something that most people would be too afraid to even try. So here's what you do, choose to leave those people behind and continue to move forward while paying closer attention to those who are for you rather then against you. To those who have scrolled past my post and shared the next persons, and to those who have unfollowed me; continue to ignore me when I make it too.

Over the years I've noticed that my contact list and my friends list on social media have decreased drastically. From friends, to schoolmates, and surprisingly (not really) even family. Sometimes I begin to blame myself for this due to the fact that I went through a very depressive stage in my life which caused me to up and move to a different state and to even lose contact with people on my own. But then I snapped back into reality, and reminded myself that it was ME who was going through something; if people were really concerned about where I was then I would've heard from them regardless. Now don't get me wrong, I too can lose contact with people often but only if it's what I need to do.

If you're someone that knows me personally, you would already know that my heart is bigger than anything in this world. I care for any and every one even if they're someone that did me wrong. Having hate in my heart is just something that I cannot live with. In my opinion, it hurts you more to stay mad at someone then it hurts them. Something I've learned along this journey is that for every person that had fallen out of my village, there were better ones put in place.

From time to time I switched schools and I moved around for the last almost six years of my life. As I moved around I started to meet a lot of different people being that I was always in school and that I always had a job no matter where it was that I resided. I would always be nice to everyone and it felt like everyone enjoyed my presence. Some people would get annoyed by me, but that's because I wasn't miserable or unhappy like they may have been. This part of my life was important to me because I met some of the greatest people ever, and some of them have become a special part of my life just within a matter of months from knowing them. Let's take my best friend for example.

In August of last year I had met this girl at school and we both had no idea what was happening with Brightwood College. Everything that drove me insane, drove her insane. Eventually we decided to switch numbers and use each other as buddies in school. As time went on we started to grow with each other and ended up becoming each other's support systems. Although we met through school she ended up becoming a friend to me and I knew she'd always be there when I needed her (even when it was dark in the parking lot and I was afraid to walk out alone.) We parked our cars next to each other every day and if either of us were missing from school, everyone would ask us where the other was because that's just how tight we had become. School is now over and she is still my girl, she's now one of my two best friends. She keeps me going when I send her a message letting her know that I'm on the verge of giving up, and she makes me laugh in those moments when I need it the most. What makes her my best friend for sure is that she checks on my son more than any of my lifelong friends have ever thought to. Remember, I've only known this individual for a year come next month and she has become a big factor in my life over this short period of time. She is my person, and I am her person.

Get you a person like her.

It never matters how long you may have known someone, it is all about what that person brings to the table in your life. Sometimes people seem to believe that you can never get to know someone in a short period of time but, someone that you meet today can have a bigger impact on your life then someone you've known forever. When you're beginning to find a foundation for your village always start with the ones that you know you can depend on forever. If someone has been absent from your life for quite some time this may not be someone that you would want to call on when you're pursing your goals. The person you're looking to call first is the one that has been consistent even when you had nothing going for yourself. Always remember the ones who were with you when you had nothing because those are the ones that love you for you. Take some time to reevaluate your friends and family before you make the decision to include them in on what it is that you're trying to do. Those people in your life that tend to throw shade in a jokingly way are NOT the ones that deserve a spot on your success journey.

Choose the ones that are honest and straightforward with you over the other individual any day. It is very hard to accept the fact that some of the people who you thought were really for you are now really against you. Again, there are a lot of people around you that may seem like they're all for you when you're on the same page as them; but when you're about to level up it starts a fire inside of them. People begin to make you feel as if you can't do what it is that you want to do because they've never done it before. Or, these people may even be the ones to unfollow you when you begin to prosper and to show off what it is that you're about to make of yourself. It's okay to leave these people behind because in reality they were not for you anyway.

Stay focus and continue to look towards the ones that had your back from the beginning even if the beginning was just a few months ago. You never know how someone really feels about you until you're doing better than them.

The Ace card in the game of life is a significance of your team because without them you probably wouldn't be able to do it all on your own. Everyone needs somebody even if they feel as if they are all that they have. When things in life tend to go wrong, we always turn to someone to try and get them to understand what it is that we're going through. Someone in your life is your go to even if you may not realize it and you must always remember that this person is there; or else you'll wind up falling apart. Ever sit in your room alone at times and feel as if the world is falling down on you?

These are the moments when your go to should be available and this is when you should try to talk to someone before drowning in your own thoughts. As a person who struggles with clinical depression I can be someone that testifies to the fact of the matter which is, having friends makes it easier. For the last few years I always told myself that I never needed anyone and that I'd always be okay without having any family or friends.

But I must say, after gaining my prayer sister and my other top 4's, life has changed for me drastically. Over the past eight years of my life I have had thoughts of attempting suicide maybe four to five times each year and let me tell you; that is the scariest moment of your life. There were times when I would drive over the bridge getting into Long Branch from Little Silver, New Jersey and I'd have to stop because thoughts of jumping over that bridge crossed my mind. There were nights when I'd have an anxiety attack and it felt as if someone was choking me to death because I couldn't even feel myself breathing anymore.

Now with my prayer sister and my friends around me, I can honestly count the amount of times that I've had suicidal thoughts leaving me with a total of zero. As soon as I begin to feel myself choke up, I pick up that phone and text the first person that I can get to in my inbox. Usually when I do this I can honestly say, my top 4's are always available and right on time. If they're not available, they'll STILL respond letting me know to just please breathe and to remember how far it is that I have come. Without those that I have chosen to be a part of my village Lord knows where I would be today.

It has changed my life tremendously by just choosing to allow people to be there for me and to understand that there are individuals in this world who actually appreciate and adore my presence. To my top 4 I say thank you; not only for being a part of my life, but for also saving my life. Without you all I probably wouldn't even have had the chance to be here and to write this book.

After sharing my story about the changes from not having a village to having a village, I hope it can impact someone else's choices about feeling like you're alone. Now a days it is very hard to trust anyone and to also choose the right people. But with time, the right people will come along and you must give them the chance to show you that you are appreciated. When choosing who to have on your team, be mindful of the fact that these people will have characteristics that make them different from the others who've pretended to be a part of your team.

The ones that belong in your village will have characteristics such as the ones below:

They'll be cheering for you even when you're thinking of doing something that seems impossible.

Whenever you need them, this person will be available as soon as they have the chance.

You can go a few days without talking to this person, but find yourself needing them and it'll feel like you've still been in contact every day.

This person will check in on you at random times just to make sure that you're doing okay on any day.

Find these people out there in the world and invite them to be a part of your village. If you have people like this in your life right now, then allow those people to be your people. Never stop a good person from being great to you because in the end it could potentially change your life. If someone you know crossed your mind just now and they are no longer a part of your life by choice, make it right and fix things because this person deserves you. In life we tend to fight and argue but it is never worth falling out and never falling back in with someone that has had a tremendous impact on your life. Time goes by very quickly and none of us have seemed to come with an expiration date that is visible to the world. Therefore, make it right with that person and choose to fix things not only for them but for yourself because nine times out of ten you may need this person. If this person carries any of the characteristics like my people up top then that means they're one of the good ones. Give them another chance and choose to make it right today.

I have another story to share with you.

One of the people in my village is someone that I met during my time in middle school. In middle school people would say that we were the best of friends and you could never find us separated for long. This person had my back always and when someone put her down or put me down it was as if it hurt both of us. We were inseparable both in school and at our homes. We basically became sisters over time and we knew each other both in and out. My friend ended up moving far away by the time we started high school and I hadn't heard from her since. After many years had went by I begun to see her name pop up on my social media pages and I was hearing things about her being back in town again. I paid it all no mind though being that we hadn't been in touch for so long. One day I was in target with my mom and all of a sudden there was my friend with her mom. It was a pretty awkward moment being that we probably both had the same things running through our minds.

She hadn't reached out to me and I hadn't reached out to her so who knows if we were even still friends at that point. I didn't really appreciate the way she acted when I saw her in target so I just let her be. Time went by again and I got an inbox from her on Facebook, which was the day when it all rekindled back to when we were in middle school. From that message and forward we begun to grow all over again. She was one of the first people to find out that I was pregnant because I decided to share the news with her and every day after that she checked up on me and the baby. Here we are a year later and this person is one out of my two BEST friends. She has been consistent with being a part of both mine and my son's life and I couldn't thank her enough for all that she's done for me.

Whenever we are in town visiting she's always right there coming to see us and always willing to spend time with us. She is my go to whenever I need quick advice, and she even still laughs at everything that I say even if it isn't funny. If I would've allowed the attitude that I thought she had given me at target determine if I responded to her message on Facebook, we probably still wouldn't be speaking till this day. I chose to give her the benefit of doubt and now here we are building a relationship that is even stronger than the one that we had in middle school.

Thank you for being you best friend.

If you have someone like this in your life, begin to try and mend this relationship because who knows if this person can be the potential missing piece to your puzzle. Who we are starts with where we come from and who we have around us. Choose the right teammates to be a part of your village and be sure to use them for the purpose of keeping you intact with being the best that you can be. You are a queen or a king, and you must always carry yourself in a proper manner along with having other kings and queens to stand beside you. Surround yourself with people that have the same mindset as you and the ones that want to win just like you.

Never settle for the friends that are against your success because those are the ones that'll try and hold you back from whatever it is that you're trying to do. Always remember to keep a village around that is for you and not against you because those are the ones that'll continuously push you to be better. We always have to pay close attention to people because not everyone is meant to be a part of your life. Some people come into your life and they're only there to teach you a quick lesson. Others may be put into your life and they may be the ones that are meant to stay in it forever. Never forget that not everyone is supposed to stick around to see your good days; some people just don't deserve to witness your greatness. It is okay if you lose a friend or two as you begin to grow because nine times out of ten those people weren't supposed to be around anyway. Take some time to really evaluate the ones around you and to see who has brought the most to your table. The ones that have kept you going on those bad days, deserve a spot in your village. The ones who you know you can turn to even if you've gone days without talking recently they deserve a spot in your village.

Distinguish the difference between who is for you and who is against you by paying attention to what they say or do about what it is that you're working on. Just like I've experienced some rough patches with people after starting my blog, you may experience the same things after you read this book and try your best to be better. I now know who both is for and against me during this process and I can tell because there's a difference in the way that both groups of people tend to treat me.

The people that have been rooting for me from the beginning are the same ones that are showing love now. There are a lot of individuals who I have done a lot for in life that aren't even taking the time to acknowledge the fact that I am actually doing something good. These individuals are the same ones that I knew from the beginning weren't really a part of my team. I've been watching their likes and comments on my pages, I've been listening to what they say when I am around them and nine times out of ten all that I have gotten is red flags. The people that I am referring to are the same ones who used to say that they cannot wait to see me win. Now that I am on the verge of winning, to them this isn't major because it means that I'll be ahead of them in life. You can never get too far ahead of people, or else they'll count you out for success.

No one wants to see you get ahead if they aren't trying to get ahead themselves. Never allow this to stop you or to slow you down because with or without these people life must go on. You have to continue to focus on your village and always choose to bring your mind back to the ones that are for you and who can keep you going even if it means that you'll get ahead of them. Whenever you feel as if people are shifting their energy into a different direction as you continue to grow, use it as a tool in your life and motivation to keep going. Instead of being sad about the lack of support, use the absence of some to make room for others who are ready to see you make it to the top. Use the spaces that you free up in your life to make room for the ones that can actually benefit you and bring something to your table. Never leave people in positions of close friends or supporters in the beginning if you see that half way to the end they're no longer around. We are kings and queens and it is destined for us to be the best that we can be. Unfortunately when we choose to hold on to the ones that are not for us then they can become a distraction and a road block in our journey of success as well. Always remember that life goes on and never allow anyone to stop you from holding your head up high. With or without some people you will forever be the best and as a king or queen nothing or no one can stop you from getting to where it is that you are destined to be.

Chapter 4: Being a Queen

In a card game you'll find that a "Queen" card is in the top four ranking for cards that have a lot of value. When it comes to figuring out what your worth is, it is important to remember that you are only worth what you make yourself worth. At times we may forget that people are very observant of how we carry ourselves and what they get from looking at us both on the inside and out. A queen carries herself with class and dignity. A woman who is a partner to a ruler in a kingdom is always looked upon as lucky. Every woman wants to be the queen, but being a queen requires a lot from a person. I myself am a Leo which is a lion, a queen of the jungle. The characteristics that are used to describe a Leo woman have a big emphasis on who we are as individuals.

The element of my sign is fire which can mean that I am fearless and I am strong. We carry ourselves with pride and we are very self-confident. The lioness can be very arrogant and stubborn, but the heart on us is twice the size of an average heart. We can be very protective over our loved ones and open to anything that comes our way. I personally am devoted to all of my responsibilities in life and I am an inspiration to others. As a Leo woman it is not easy to keep up our image, but we sure make it look as if it is. Sometimes I find myself struggling with my weaknesses such as how strong my ego can be and how impatient I can get at times. But, I never fall too short of being the best that I can be.

Although most of you may not be Leo's, you are all still fiercely and wonderfully made. The same characteristics and traits that a Leo woman holds can be the same for you Aries, Taurus, or Aquarius. Whatever your zodiac symbol is can be a sign of who you are, but each of us make us who we are. Practicing on yourself to see what you are like is the first step in determining if you are a true king or queen. As your value in life begins to increase, you are expected to become a better person every step of the way.

When you become a mother or a father you are expected to become a better leader to set an example for your children. When you become a CEO or a principal of a school, the business is expecting you to hold the accountability of being responsible for your business. No matter how far you go in life, there will always be someone watching you and checking to see if you're up for whatever it is that you're going to face in life. Sometimes it may seem like people hold you to a bit of a high standard just because of who you are as a person, but this does not have to always be the case.

In 2014 I was the president of my freshmen class in college. Getting into this position seemed to be very easy for me because all I had to do was get majority of the voters to vote for me and socializing was always my thing so I had no problem. Once in the position, everything had changed for me. I was no longer just a freshmen class student; I was the PRESIDENT of the freshmen class. My name and face was plastered on to the front page of the newspaper the next morning and it was all over the social media pages as well. I had become well known overnight and everyone would look at me as the president, not just Jazz anymore. Over time I enjoyed holding this position because as a Leo I love to be the center of attention along with being the natural born leader that I am. It all seemed so easy from attending meetings, to leading meetings, and doing whatever else the book of student council required me to do. It was coming to me naturally, being the class president was something simple that I could probably carry with me for the next four years of my time here at school.

I was wrong.

It begun to get overwhelming. It was as if I couldn't be myself anymore. I was unable to be like my friends and to get into things that college students usually get into. When I went out with my friends I had to carry myself in a manner that showed that I was still in the role of a president. When events would happen at school I couldn't get up on stage and have fun with the other girls because then my reputation would have been ruined. Who would've thought, even if you were on your best behavior there's this thing called rumors that outweighed what people saw. What people heard about you seemed to become more of a trend rather than what they seen you do. One day a friend of mine in class logged on to this new blogging site that was created to bash students at the college. She scrolled through and managed to make it to a page that she said made her angry. At first I didn't understand where her anger was coming from but then I saw the words "Freshmen Class President." There were a list of things posted on this page about me with some being true and others just being false accusations based off of what people had heard about me.

I was devastated. It crushed me to know that people saw me the way that they did and it changed my whole outlook on the position that I held. Being that I had already previously suffered with depression and anxiety, this situation had then sent my emotions through the roof. I couldn't believe that holding this power had meant so much to people that they'd go as far as crushing my reputation. It was as if I had just lost my dignity and it was never coming back. Whether if I said things were true or false no one believed me because it was more entertaining to believe the lies then to try and hear what I thought about myself. It came to a point where I just couldn't take it anymore. I knew that allowing the people to win and allowing them to see me fall wasn't an option, but I was already fighting a battle that I couldn't win. Depression. As if I didn't already feel bad about myself, the people ended up winning because their words just cut that deeply. I got out of this position. I couldn't take it anymore and I just wanted to be free and happy like every other freshman at school. If it weren't for my depression I'm sure I could've took those sharp knives that were thrown at me and turned them around to throw them right back at the people but it was hard. I just couldn't find the strength to be strong enough to take all of the mess that came with being the class president any longer.

After giving up my spot, it was like a breath of fresh air. No one was concerned about me anymore, they started paying closer attention to whoever it was that took over my spot in the meantime. Although everything that was posted on that blog had become a part of me now, I didn't care anymore because there was no reason for me to ever feel like I was doing something wrong. Whatever choices and decisions I made they were no longer a reflection of the class president. If I wanted to go to the illegal frat parties I could, if I wanted to drink on campus property and run from the campus patrol I could. It felt good to finally get the real experience of a college student before my freshmen year had come to an end. I tell this story to remind you all of the fact of the matter which is that no matter what you try and become in life there will forever be those who are praying on your downfall. Yes I failed at staying strong and yes I allowed the people to push me to the point of getting out of that seat; but that was because I let my depression win. When we struggle with battles such as depression the roller coaster doesn't feel the same. It's more painful and the weight of the wind becomes very heavy over your mind and body. There was no way that I could manage being the president and wanting to live freely at the same time when life was already a battle for me.

Time has gone on and I am now working on becoming a full time blogger with a wealthy income. This time around, things are DIFFERENT. My depression hasn't went away but over the years I have grown extensively and I have transformed from a freshmen in college to a young woman with a goal. Although some people believe that the past will haunt you forever, I honestly can say that my past has changed me forever. People may remember me as the girl who dropped out of college her freshmen year, but you can be certain that after this book launch I will go down in the same books as the young successful black woman who managed to write and publish a book in just three weeks. Being a queen is not easy, but it can look that way at times.

Even though I gave up once, I have never allowed myself to give up again. No matter how many times depression has tried to stop me or to slow me down, I've kept pushing on and making my way through the game. Sometimes we tend to let our crowns tip over when we cry, but we never let it fall. We always catch our crown before it hits the ground and then we wipe our tears and keep going. Whether if you are a queen or a king I want you to pay attention to my stories to help with shifting yours into the right direction. When life gets you to a point where you become discouraged and worried about what others may think, you must stop and remember who you are. Never allow yourself to give up like I did. Although this is bound to happen maybe once or twice, continue to pursue what it was that you were pursuing and never let anything get in the way of your success. There may be trials and tribulations that are implemented in your life to slow you down like a skip card in a game of Uno, but always remember that your turn will come back around again. What you do with that next turn that you are given is up to you. The best thing for you to do is to take that turn and reverse it all the way around into something better than what it was that you may have failed at.

Yes I ended up dropping out of college because of all that I was going through, and yes I may not have my psychology degree right now; but the most important thing is that I am living to tell my story. If I would've continued on with the fight that I was fighting I am more than certain that my situation at that time would've been the cause for me to end my life early. Being that I am here to tell my story to you all and to prevent you from giving up means more to me than anything in this world. I am glad that I can now use that tiring and dreading time of my life to come and help the next person to remember how much they are worth.

We are all given different challenges in life and some may be harder than others. But there is no challenge that is worse than facing the fact that you may struggle from a mental disorder. Some of us may not believe in disorders, but they are real and we face them every day. Whenever you begin to feel as if your crown is slipping or that you can no longer go on it means that you are struggling with a battle that may not be clear to you yet. When it comes to figuring out what the underlining problem may be that is holding you back, we sometimes brush it off and look right past the problem. When you feel as if there is something wrong then go with your instinct and face the truth which is that something is wrong. A lot of people in my village personally struggle with reality and facing the truth.

Although the people in my village struggle with understanding that there is a problem occurring in their lives, I have faced my truths and gotten help for what it is that I struggle with. I not only struggle with clinical depression and anxiety, but I struggle with everyday living and trying to be the best mother that I can be. Life itself is a battle and it is a battle that'll try and steal your crown and your value away from you. When those in my village tend to slip away from their inner beauty and worth, I drift them back in a direction that reminds them of who they are and what they are capable of doing. At times we may have a chip on our shoulder that tells us that everything won't be okay, but in the end you will always come out stronger.

I never like for others to feel the pain that I feel every day so I start with those in my village and I inspire them to fight off whatever it is that they are up against. Some things can be everyday life situations, but on the other hand it can be an underlining disorder that you just haven't been aware of this entire time. It is important that we take the time to get to know ourselves in order to figure out where it is in life that we need the most help. There are plenty of sources and others around us who can help us to become better. Some of us may be afraid of the truth and afraid to admit that we have a problem but it is okay. I am here to tell you that this is something that has to be addressed before you can make the decision to be a true king or queen.

It took me years to realize that I was in need of help. I was in denial and I knew that I would get through each day one battle at a time. Being that I have experienced it I plan to help each and every one of you to stay clear of the things that I decided not to face right away. You have to start by getting the help that you need. If you are struggling with sadness and grief due to the loss of a love one then seek counseling. If you are physically incapable of getting some things done at times, then head to your doctor and get that annual physical that you have not received in a few years. Now is the time for you to begin to focus more on yourself and what may be holding you back from being the best that you can be.

Right now I'd like to take some time to bring you to a focus point where you can start to depict what the underlining problem is in your life. At times we may be so concerned about what's happening around us that we pay the slightest amount of attention to what it is that is going on right in front of us. I know that I personally put the majority of the people around me before myself. I'll be at my lowest point sometimes and I will still choose to put someone else's needs before mine. I find myself giving out money when my bills aren't even caught up at that moment. I'll see me making time for someone else's needs and realizing that if I do this for them I'll be late for whatever it is that I need to do. But, I still manage to squeeze them in causing myself stress at the end of the day. Whenever I choose to put someone else before myself I realize that I get overly exhausted and drained out pretty quickly.

Being that I never say no or complain about how helping someone makes me feel, I think these people fail to realize that I am feeling terrible.

Ever done any of these things for people and feel the same way? If you answered yes then let me remind you that you my friend can no longer choose to pour from an empty cup anymore. If we are not taking care of ourselves before we begin to take care of our loved ones then this leaves us with nothing which is what we probably started with in the first place. It is time that we put ourselves first so that we can become better and well enough to care for ourselves and everyone else as well. I'm sure most of you have devoted so much time to trying to be the best person so that everyone else can accept you and love you but that is no longer a concern. The main concern for you from this day forward is to worry about what is happening for you mentally, physically, spiritually and even emotionally.

Choose to love yourself first right now.

If you have said yes to choosing to love yourself first then I have some encouraging factors that I'd like for you to implement into your day to day living.

Factor #1: Creating a Diet

Start by creating a healthy diet for yourself which needs to include three consecutive meals a day. I know this may sound crazy but I am here to testify to the fact of the matter which is that food is the source of energy. I have begun to eat three meals a day and it has changed my everyday living drastically. I make time for breakfast in the morning even though I used to make the excuse that there wasn't enough time in the morning. I pack a lunch each day so that I know for sure that I have a lunch and I never have to worry about having money or going out of my building to find something to eat within an hour. Every night at dinner I sit down at the table and I make sure that I eat a decent amount of food in order to fill me up for the night. To make this happen you have to begin with making a schedule and finding the time to assure yourself that you'll be able to get all three of these meals in. Trust me, you'll begin to see a difference.

Factor #2: Begin to Say No

This seems to be the hardest factor of them all but it has definitely helped me with finding the time to take care of myself more often. When people continuously ask you to do things for them, there comes a point where you just have to say no. Try it. Although it may hurt you to tell that friend or family member that you cannot drive to where they need to be today, realize that this leaves you with time to get something done for yourself. Everyone else's situation is not your fault. If someone asks you for money because they're without a job and you don't have it, be sure to say no. Never scrape up money for someone else knowing that you don't even have it for yourself. Your savings is YOUR savings, so never touch it unless it is an emergency. I've learned this the hard way and I've ended up on the verge of losing my car plenty of times before because I dipped into my already saved payment to help someone that didn't even plan on paying me back. Begin to say no to the things that can throw you off track and get in the way of where it is and what you're trying to do right now.

Factor #3: Spend Time Alone

Start finding the time that you need in order to spend it with yourself. Yes I know we have children and we have responsibilities that require us to never get the time but those right there are excuses. At some point during the week you have to go grocery shopping, right? Stop inviting your husband and the kids or your mom to go with you; take that moment and spend it alone. When you're at work it's always nice to catch up on the latest gossip at lunch time but every once in a while each week, separate yourself from everyone else and spend time eating your favorite meal or outside with nature. Leave your Facebook feed alone and check back in later on in the day. We are given thirty minutes and sometimes an hour to do whatever it is that we please. Take that time and write in a journal, read a chapter of a book that you love, or even go for a walk outside and become one with nature. We all tend to make excuses for why we cannot get our alone time but trust me, it is possible if you just believe and find a will in a way.

Factor #4: From Hobby to Passion

Now this one is something major, something that may even be able to change your life just like mine is about to change. I used to spend most of my days talking with other people, encouraging them to be better, and responding to their questions on advice that they may have needed. So, one day I made the decision to turn all of what I discuss with people and all of what I go through personally into a blog. At first I could only relate to what I go through as a clinically depressed mother, but now it's as if my life situations are touching the hearts of many other people as well. This blogging thing can take me very far in life, by helping me to go from an overly hardworking mother to a stay at home and doing what I love mama. So, I want you all to do the same.

Point out something that you're passionate about, something that you notice yourself to do every day. Whether it be: surfing the online internet for the latest fashion trends, writing song lyrics or making beats, cooking up a good meal every evening, writing in your journal each day, or even being a parent. All of those ideas are hobbies that can easily turn into something that you're passionate about. Use what it is that you're good at and make it a part of your everyday life. Create a cookbook full of your favorite recipes and connect with amazon kindle to get paid for it in an eBook format. Create a video or a snippet of you singing or rapping that song that you want the world to hear and put it up on YouTube along with a ton of other videos forming your own YouTube channel. Take your journal entries and anonymously post them on a blogging site that you will create to share your stories with someone that may be looking for advice or someone to relate to. DO SOMETHING! Try something different for once guys, and make a living off of what it is that you love.

All of the following four factors may not be something that you're comfortable with trying, but guess what? Being comfortable means that you're content with where you are in life and I'm sure that's not the truth. Shift back to the thought of how you are a king or queen and how strong you are. We are fearless individuals and we must pay close attention to the opportunities that are offered to us. It takes the least amount of time to get out into the real world and to show your face. Although you may be afraid of failure and afraid of not getting the publicity that you need at times, you never know what you may get. Take a risk and try something different for once. Never allow your fear to stop you from possibly making the greatest decision that you could ever make for yourself. Use the following three factors to increase your worth as a king or a queen and begin by transforming and blossoming into something great.

There are people in this world today who started by just doing something. Look at the kid who created "The Shiggy Challenge." All he had to do was create a choreography, promote himself to the world, and now he's sitting on millions of dollars because this was Drake's way of saying thank you for making his song hit the top of the charts (at least he was supposed to be). It didn't take much. He didn't have to spend thousands of dollars on a video shoot or go online and invest in other companies to make a way. He used INSTAGRAM which is free, FACEBOOK which is free, a VILLAGE to back him up which is FREE. This is a perfect example of how we can begin to use what we have to get what it is that we want.

Whenever you get discouraged or second guess if you should post something, share something, or telling somebody about it, remember that the only way you'll make it is if you do something about it. After reading this chapter I hope you all have gained some clarity on how to notice your king or queen characteristics. Whatever it is that may be holding you back from being the best that you can be, I hope you spend less time focusing on that. Invest in the things that matter from this day forward, and spend time doing something in order to get to where it is that you want to be in life.

I failed multiple times, but I am here now living to tell my story and I even may have the chance to make it based off of this. Never be afraid of failure for it is the number one attribute that contributes to us never making it to the top. Use what you have as an advantage and make a change for yourself by actually taking the time to invest in you and whatever it is that you're good at. We are given options in life, along with a host of choices and decisions that we can make. When we begin to pay more attention to the opportunities and the ways that we can start an investment it becomes clearer to us in order to see what it is that we may be good at or passionate about. Just like a card game, you can keep playing on until someone wins.

There are over hundred cards that come in a box and each of those can end up being yours at some point. Use what you can to get what it is that you want. The internet is the biggest source for it all because it is free and has a lot of answers for us. Take that alone time to surf the web and find the steps on how to make your dreams come true. There are answers for everything out there and you can be the first to find them if you take the time to go ahead and DO IT. Stop spending time thinking what if or maybe and begin to realize that anything is possible. If I never teach you all anything in life I'd like for you to remember that we are kings and queens and we can conquer the world if we really try to. Create a village and a team to back you up with what it is that you want to do. Spend some time out of the twenty four hours that you're given in a day to research and find ways to make it happen. As a king or as a queen you have enough value and worth to make something out of yourself and to see change with just making decisions to be better.

In chapter five we will discuss the importance of the many opportunities and chances that we are given in life. Just like a card game, there are plenty of ways to make it to that winner title as long as you commit your time and your mind to figuring out the way the game works. Use what you have learned in chapter four to change and try something different.

Chapter 5: Drawing an Ace through King

In a card game you get the chance of flipping and changing thirteen options worth of cards. In life, the cards that we have are the opportunities that are out there for us to take each day. During my twenty two years of living, I have come across a large amount of options as far as what it was that I wanted to do in life. As time went on I struggled with staying committed to something, and I also struggled with understanding how this game of life worked.

In 2015 I was given the chance to complete an internship with ICMA-RC in Washington, DC. At this location I was told to sit at a computer desk and talk to people, insert data, file paperwork for hours at a time, and to do whatever office work was needed to be done from previous months and years. At first this was a cool deal for me because in exchange I was receiving $900-$1200 checks every two weeks that began to make me feel real good.

Now keep in mind I was only 19 years old four years ago so receiving checks like that every two weeks meant, spending and splurging on whatever it was that I wanted. Instead of me being smart and saving my earnings, I was too young to understand that the money I was receiving was now real income and that I needed to invest in myself. I also didn't understand that this was an opportunity that only came once in a lifetime and with not knowing this I decided to turn down the position being that I preferred not to be in an office setting all day. This wasn't the smartest move that I've ever made in life but it definitely taught me a life lesson which was to appreciate the chances that you are given.

It is now 2018 and I have been given another great opportunity which can be life changing for me. I am now employed with the number one hospital in the state of Maryland and a hospital that is on the charts worldwide; Johns Hopkins Bayview Medical Center. During the hiring process with Hopkins I continuously grew anxious every time something would come my way via email or phone call. While waiting for the final say so, I was on an externship that was needed for my medical assistant program. I completed my externship in a pediatric office as one of two medical assistants and thanks to the other MA, I finally received that "Congratulations" phone call from my lovely current supervisor. It never seems to amaze me how quickly time can fly by.

This process seemed as if it took forever but it actually took no time at all for that start date to come up. Now that I have started my employment here it's as if the days have become longer. Before this job, I was a waitress and never got the chance to sit down for too long. Just like the job in DC I am back to being an adult and working a 9-5pm each and every day. Although I LOVE my job, my coworkers, and my patients, it feels as if this life just isn't for me for the second time. The opportunities that I have been receiving are amazing and they have had big impacts on my life, but I always knew that there was more out there for me. When playing a card game, you never pay attention to the cards that may not seem beneficial for what it is that you're trying to accomplish so you throw them out and try something else.

I want to be rich.

That is what I am trying to accomplish for both my son and I within the next five years. So, here I am throwing away cards and finding other ways to win. Writing a book is not something that happens overnight, but it is something that can happen fairly quickly. One night on Pinterest I came across a pin that said *"How to Start a Blog from Absolute Scratch"* by the "Twins Mommy". After reading this blog I decided to give it a try because it seemed like something that could benefit me. After scrolling through I began to read how she became a stay at home mom and then she also left me with a list of other bloggers incomes that had grew extensively within a matter of just a few months. *"Abby from Just a Girl and Her Blog-$40,124 in one month, Leana from What a Mommy Does-$9,997 in one month."* The list continued on and my eyes began to widen so far that I was able to use them for rearview mirrors at this point.

I COULDN'T BELIEVE IT!

All it took was for me to scroll through Pinterest one night and to come across this blog for my mind to shift in a totally different direction. Again, choosing a card between an Ace and a King.

Starting this blogging career became very easy over time, and it was to the point where I have now done the following:

Launched a blog in JUST 5 days.

Begun to write a book, which will be published in 3 weeks' time.

Signed up with Amazon Kindle to begin making some income off of everything that I have now decided to do.

Now let's keep in mind that I am a CLINICALLY depressed, full time employee, and a twenty one year old mother who is making this all happen so fairly quickly. Even though there are times during this process when I can just rip my hair out of my head; I keep going. There are nights when I am extremely exhausted after bed and bath time and all I want to do is sleep. But guess what? Instead, I keep going. I continue to invest in myself almost every day devoting some time and some money to what it is that I am doing. I never let the days go by without me doing something to contribute to this future that I am in the process of creating for myself. If some of you just read that and said, "This is impossible, no one could every do this", I am here to be your testifier because I AM DOING IT! I have a goal guys, and in order to accomplish that goal it is my duty to serve and to do whatever it is that I must do to make sure that I complete it. Even though there may be times when you feel as if you can't just start something, remind yourself that the only way something will get done is if you begin to play.

Take a moment and think about something that you'd really like to see happen for yourself. Whether it be growing rich, earning an extra income, or making that new hobby of yours go viral. Now think about what it is that would be required of you to make this happen, then think about where to start. If you just read that and thought "I have no idea." Then there are still no excuses BECAUSE I had no idea how to create a website, no idea how to create an eBook template, or how to write one hundred pages worth of text. But, here I am writing one hundred pages worth of text and viewing my websites viewers every now and then to see who has visited my site. Although I could have made excuses for myself and decide to just figure it out later, it was my choice to figure it out NOW and to make it happen right away. Playing with the cards that I've been dealt and making a way out of no way. Although we may have thirteen options in a card game, when those cards are flipped over in that deck, we never know what may be coming next. Even though there are many options out there as to what you can do in life, you must first figure out what it is that you actually want.

When I think about that deck of cards, I think about the process that I've went through to get to where it is that I'm planning to go. There are many different resources out there that can either help you, or slow you down. This right here is that deck of cards because picking a card is basically trial and error. It is very risky to pick up a card and not know what it's going to be but in order to keep the game going you kind of have no choice. Being that I want to keep my game going, I have picked through many different cards and threw them out or kept them in my hand for when I might actually be ready to use them.

As a new blogger and new author, there are many different steps that you must take in order to reach Abby and Lena's goals which remember is thousands of dollars' worth of income each week. Making the decision to commit to this new idea is the first step. Before you can move forward with something you must always decide if that thing is right for you and if you can actually commit to everything that is expected of you during the process. After deciding that you're all in then you must take the time to do your research and to find answers to all of the questions that you may have. Taking time out to do research can be tough only because it requires time that we may not have. When you really want something to happen trust me that time will appear without you even noticing. It becomes a passion for you and you'll catch yourself researching tips and tricks without even thinking about it. Once I chose to become dedicated and committed to blogging, I started to find myself on Pinterest at many different times of the day just looking up tips on how to grow my blog or how to get the most money and time out of it. I never go a day without investing in my new passion, I always find the time to get something done that contributes to my new choice.

Find what it is that you're passionate about.

Take that something that you are passionate about and see if you can turn it into a hobby. This can be anything from the following:

Taking photographs of nature

Talking to people

Cooking with new recipes

Writing music and singing songs

Everything on that list above can potentially make you money and you may not have even known that. A photographer is always needed because people are always looking for images to post or to share. Talking to people can be your passion and you can transform that into becoming a life coach who makes millions or even a motivational speaker who travels the world and makes millions of dollars as well. Cooking is something that most women do every week of their lives and some of them are very good at what they do. Women who love to cook can turn their recipes into a book and sell it on the internet as an eBook with amazon kindle for whatever price they'd like to sell it for. Music is the key to happiness, everyone uses music and the lyrics of songs as their go to in life in order to keep them motivated. You can make your own YouTube channel if you wanted with your own music, or you can use your social media as a networking tool to get what you've created in the right hands of someone important.

Use the cards that you have been given and transform your life into something great. Everything in life that you're good at can become a talent. From being the best hair braider, to being the most flexible person in the world, whatever it is that you are good at can make you rich someday. Everything that we find interest in can be a brand attached to our name. We can use the talents that we have and take them with us wherever we go by networking and using our social sites to connect us with others. Never fear the game for there are so many options that you'll have to help you along the way.

The opportunities that we are given in life come our way for many reasons. Even when you feel as if something may not have been meant for you there was something in that moment that benefited your future. Whether if you spent time at a job that you hated and made a lot of money from it to save, or if you met someone at a new salon for the first time and they showed interest in what it is that you do. No matter where you go in life always expect something good and bad to come out of it because you can never take the good without the bad or the bad without the good. There will be challenging phases during your time of trying to win the game, but the most important thing is that you play your cards right and you use all of the options that you have before trying to win. Play the game smart, and never pay too much attention to what it is that your opponent is trying to do.

Although you may not want to be the next blogger or find interest in what it is that I am doing, take the time to think about something you've been doing every day and didn't even realize was a talent. Some of the ideas that you may have in mind can seem impossible to transform into a career, but you'd be surprised by the answers that google can offer you when you believe and do your research.

When I was in high school I always loved the days when a motivational speaker was coming in to speak to my class. I loved those days because at this time the individuals were truly motivational for me because I someday wanted to become a speaker as well. I would listen to everything that they'd say and I would turn their advice into something bigger. Whatever advice they gave us, I would use it and then change it into something that was more relatable as to what it was that I was going through in life. It was nice to hear some of the things that they would say because it brought some positive energy and light to my mind and dark days.

After the assemblies were over I would go to lunch or the next period of the day and do some research, the search engine tool that I would always turn to was google. Google is the best thing that was ever created because it gives you so many different tools and links to use in order to figure out what it is that you would like to know. As I used the search engine to find information on "How to Be a Motivational Speaker" it began to lead me to other motivational speakers that I may not have met in person but they were there on the web and available for me to listen to. Google would take me to different websites and even videos on YouTube to listen to other people's stories and journeys on how they got to become a motivational speaker.

I enjoyed watching the videos and I enjoyed using my new search engine tool to help me with putting the pieces together on how to be a motivational speaker. Unfortunately I let go of this dream and gave up on figuring out how it was done. At times it would get boring and I would doubt myself when it came to how someone else made it to where they are right now. I never thought I could meet someone that could help me with getting publicity and I never saw myself traveling the world or finding the time to invest in myself because my focus then was graduating high school and starting my college career.

Now here I am eight years later and I've found something else that I'm interested in turning into a platform on my journey of success. I use google and Pinterest to find all of the answers to the steps that I must take to grow my current blog. I take the advice that I am given and I use it even if it is boring or a hard task that I'm not interested in. I do all of this because this is what I want and anything that I want is able to become possible by starting with myself and me doing what I have to do.

Find the tools out there that can help you to grow and transform whatever you're currently working on into something bigger. Use all of your resources and never make an excuse as to why you cannot get something done. Most things in life tend to be all about who you know rather than what it is that you know. We must continue to use those ace through king cards in our deck and hold on to the ones that can change our lives for the better. Always take down someone's information if you think they can contribute to your future.

Never be afraid to ask questions if you're in the audience of someone that you need to get more information from (that was me when the speakers were at my high school.) The tools that you use can go in your hand to be a part of your moves in life but always remember that you do not have to hold on to them forever. You can switch those cards out with another and see if that other might be better for you.

Being that you never know what might be coming next in life, always choose to hold on to as many resources as you can. Although in a card game eventually you have to let all of your cards go, in life we have enough room and space for anything that can help us to become better. If the talent that you have chosen to help you grow can really change your life, then begin to show it to the world.

You never have to start big when it comes to introducing something new to people, start with right where you are. Use the people who are around you now and see what they think about what you're about to bring into the world. Pick up the card of faith and step out on that first, so that you can get a feeling of security. Once you become confident and get feedback on how great your talent is, then it becomes easier for you to believe that this something can be the change that you needed in your life. Some of you may be making this decision just to have a little bit more income on the side and that is perfectly fine.

Whatever you decide is up to you because the outcome from taking this chance in the first place will be based off of your decision. Even if you begin to feel like it may not work during the process, revert back to your many different options and try something else because giving up is not an option. Having opportunities and options to choose from can make anything possible in life. It is all up to you to decide what you will do with those things whether if it be to use them or to throw them away like the cards you thought may not have been any good for you. Sometimes we throw away cards not even realizing that we may need them later on down the road. If it looks like it cannot contribute to your success based off of its worth compared to all of the other cards in that moment, then we usually just get rid of it. With that being said I must tell you something important, which is to never judge a book by its cover in life.

After starting my new job I began to network with a lot of the individuals in the office to see what they were like. Some of them seemed to be very far off from the friends that I have at home so I decided to not even waste my time interacting with them anymore. They would talk about things that I had no idea about and plus everyone here was older than me so I couldn't relate to most of the things that they go through. I started to stay to myself after I attempted to get to know them, but then one day I overheard a conversation in the office next to me. Two employees were talking and I overheard one say, "By the way, I enjoyed your website and I am loving where you're headed with your blog."

Lightbulb.

A lightbulb lit up in my mind and it was then when I realized that someone in this office could relate to what it is that I am trying to do right now. Although I had no idea what her website or blog may have been about I already knew her process had to be similar to mind. I decided to give this opportunity a chance because in that moment I had no idea what could've came out of me taking that chance. I went over to her office and asked her all about what is that she did. Unfortunately our blogs were nowhere near relatable but, she gave me insight on things and shared two other people with me that were inspirations for her. I now listen to their podcasts every day and whenever I need advice on making the next decision as far as my blog is concerned, I know that I can always go next door and talk to this resource that I now had.

You see what I did there?

I took a chance and used an opportunity that could've either been something good or bad. The advice that the two podcasts give me have helped me along my journey so far and if I would've never spoken to the young lady then I would've never even known that the individuals existed. Start taking chances guys and when you do, never be afraid about the chance that you may fail instead of it all turning out to be something great. Never forget about all of the options and opportunities that you may have.

Keep count of the things that come your way and start to pay closer attention to the ones that could potentially help you once you get further along in life. I know it can be intimidating to take the chances like I do (approaching a stranger who may not even want to talk to you) but it never hurts to try. With the challenges that come along with being successful you have to always consider the fact that the road may not be easy and you should take all of the help that you can get. The goal here is to continue to play in the game from beginning until the very end.

Chapter 6: Playing from Beginning to End

Have you ever started something and then decided to not even continue it? In life sometimes we begin to do things that we find to be interesting and then we never fall through with completing it. From starting a new diet to launching your first eBook like me, it is hard to understand that obstacles in life take time. When you begin to play a card game if you start to see that your opponent is on the verge of winning, it never looks good if you decide to give up and let them win.

They've been doubting you since the game started so therefore you have to hang in there and try your best to prove them wrong. Trying out new tasks in life can be discouraging especially when it's something that you've never done before; but always remember that it's better to say that you've tried then to not even attempt the task at all. When you're thinking about throwing in the towel and not moving forward with whatever you planned to pursue, just keep me in the back of your mind.

When I first finished high school I already knew that I wanted to go to college because earning a college degree was the right thing to do. I was on the right track of completing college until at the end of my freshmen year which was when I fell into that deep depressive state which caused me to drop out of school a semester early. It was very hard for me to go on every day for the last few months that I spent there. It was as if it hurt me to even think about living anymore. Years go by and I end up finding myself back at this point of trying to pursue my college degree again but this time in the state of Maryland. Not even a month into the first semester, depression rolled around again and this is when I realized that I actually had a problem that was not going away.

I spent some time alone trying to figure out what was happening with me and then I realized that I still hadn't finished what it was that I was trying to finish. Even though we sometimes feel like things HAVE to get done, there may be something in your life that is continuously holding you back and it'll feel like you have no control over it. When you start to feel this way it is important for you to reflect on the reasons behind why you feel the way that you do and move forward from there. It made me upset to continuously start over and stop multiple times but it wasn't my fault. I was trying to push through and to do everything that I could to manage and to make it through school, but I guess that it just wasn't meant for me.

Whenever you're playing in the game you have to focus on the final result after you've played for so long. People tend to rush the process and assume that things have to happen overnight but the best work always comes from those who take their time and do it right. In order to keep up with the game you have to play from beginning to end and then observe all the things that fall in between those two time periods.

Whatever it is that slows you down when you're trying to be your best replace it with some positivity. Begin to turn every challenge into a life lesson and turn it into something that helps you rather than hurts you. There have been a lot of road blocks put into my journey of success but I always find a detour around them. When I think about all of the times that I've failed or that I ended up with a negative result, they tend to always outweigh the good things that have come my way. The most important thing about this though is the amount of value that each part of the equation held. Life is like an equation. We all want to add and subtract something from it all the time but we never know what the outcome will be after we take away or bring something to our playing table.

I always thought that adding more things to my life would make it easier, but I never realized that it had to be balanced. Every time I would add something I'd hold on to what wasn't for me. When you make the decision to move forward you have to leave behind what no longer benefits the next step for you. There will be a lot of things put in place to stop you or to slow you down but the goal is for you to keep going. So, in order to keep going you have to let go of what is not meant for you and try your best to pick up what may be useful to you from the start of the game to the end. When we think about finishing and getting to where it is that we want to be, we have to consider the fact that things may not always go as planned. I tend to live my life by an outline.

Whenever I am working on something and I plan before I start, the deadline that I create has to be the deadline that I meet. No matter how stressful the situation may become I always have to get the project done when I said that I would. If I end up not completing it by this time, then it makes me feel like a complete failure. Sometimes I can be very hard on myself but it is only because I want the best for me. It gets very overwhelming when I make life harder for myself but I always end up satisfied at the end if I stick to the script. I want you all to learn from me and the way that I choose to get things done.

No matter how many times you set a deadline for something, if you do not complete it on time remember that this is okay. Not everything in life goes as planned and we cannot allow the amount of fails that we experience to stop us from finishing even if it's not the day that we planned to. When something comes up and stops you from being productive then you must push through and try your best to do it again the next day. We can never dwell on the things that happen because everything tends to happen for a reason. If there happens to be a road block that appears during your time of trying to get something done, I need you to look that roadblock in the face and challenge it to try and stop you from doing whatever it is that you're doing. Never allow the road block to keep you from going to wherever it is that you are trying to go. Find a different way around it and continue to play in your game because the goal is to make it to the end.

As you plan out important factors in your life start by realizing that they are important to you so therefore you want everything to be done right. Never rush the process because in order for it to be something great it'll have to take time. I once thought that everything in life had to happen quickly or else it will never become anything great. Then I started to realize that everything around me that had been successful was created months and years ago but it needed to be worked on. There may have been times when something was created and launched right away but the feedback and reviews on that product may not have been the best. Always see things for what they are instead of what they can potentially be. When you're more realistic about the matter then you'll realize that some things take time to create and for it the best that it can be.

The best things in life are far from free, every quantity comes with a price based off of its quality. When you're trying to stay in the game from beginning to the end, the in between stages are what have the best quality. These are the times when you're failing, succeeding, and even trying to give up. It is rich and worth a lot to us because it'll be the parts that get us to the end which is where we wanted to be since the beginning. I always knew that I wanted to be rich someday. Being that I knew this already I've taken every chance and opportunity since the beginning in order to find my way to the end. Sometimes I may feel like giving up or feel as if I just can't do it anymore but I continue to go on and move forward. The reason behind it all is because there is an endpoint to the game of life that I am trying to get to, in order to say that I've finally won.

During my four years of high school I was a part of the cheerleading squad. Sometimes the challenges would become difficult and I'd give up but then I'd attempt to try again. It was the getting up and trying again parts of the journey that kept me going. I never thought that I could be half of the cheerleader that most of the girls were because they were so good at it. I would try my best to keep up and to give it my all but there would come times when I would start to doubt myself. It was easy in the beginning but making it to the end which was senior day was the hardest part.

The reason why I doubted myself or felt as if I couldn't be good enough was because I had just had my patella (front knee ligament) repaired. When you're a cheerleader or an athlete in general your legs play a big part in everything there is that you do. It was try out season again and something told me to just go for it. Although I feared failure and didn't want to hear that I had not made the team, I being me still went out and tried. Being that I made it to my senior day, then this means that I made the team. I went in there and I gave it my all, there was a goal in my mind that I had to reach and I knew that this step would be one of the many that I would have to take in order to reach my goal. After this experience I then continued on every year that followed because I witnessed greatness and I knew that if I could get pass one roadblock, then I could get past them all.

To play from beginning to end you have to want it really badly guys. I wanted to be able to walk across the field on senior day to celebrate my victory. I wanted to make my mom proud and show her and everyone else that the knee surgery procedure that I had couldn't stop me. So what did I do? I went out and I made it happen. Begin preparing for the end by taking chances and using the opportunities that you are given to push through whatever you're going through. Even when we feel like giving up we always have to remember why it is that we started to play in the first place. When you're reminded of the why's in life you start to feel more confident about what it is that you're doing. If there is nothing in your mind that is driving you to accomplish your goal then it may cause you to lose some motivation. Find your why and then choose to stick to the process in order to get to the end. The end maybe closer than you think so plan to get ahead and to never give up or stop because you're afraid.

When it seems as if nothing is going right for us we tend to just give up and allow whatever roadblock that popped up to slow us down. It's the same as if you were driving in a car and came up on a roadblock.

One day I was driving to a big concert that I had waited weeks on and the day was finally here. As I'm driving to the location of the concert I started to notice that the traffic was building up in front of me. Apparently there had been construction going on up ahead of us so it was slowing everyone down. When I tell you that I was in traffic for over two hours, it was over two hours. The road that we were on was so busy that when the construction turned it into one lane it just made it a mess. You would think that the town would figure out a better time for construction to happen knowing that a concert was in town, but I guess they just didn't care.

I sat in that traffic for those two hours waiting to get to the concert that I was already late for, and I never thought to detour around what I had come upon. Instead of me trying to find a way out of the mess and a detour to still get to where I needed to be, I just turned around and went back home. I was very upset about missing the concert but I just couldn't take the fact that the construction had slowed me down to the point where I couldn't move at all. That was it. I didn't try to make anything happen I just gave up and turned back around to head home.

This is just like the challenges that may come upon us in life. Whenever we seem to think that something is in our way of getting to where we need to be we never find a way around it, we just turn back around and give up. Try something different in life. Try to fight back and to find the other ways that you can go in order to get to where it is that you want to be right now. Although there might be chances of failure and you may feel as if it's too hard, choose to fight back anyway. Never allow the fear of striking out to stop you, just continue to go all the way making sure that you're in the game from beginning to end.

Every time you choose to stop because you may have come across a roadblock you're also choosing to give up on what it is that you really want. In order to make it to the top you have to jump over all of the hurdles that are placed in front of you because nothing that is worth your time comes easy. When you begin to notice the challenges in life to start appearing more I can promise you that this means you're very close to the end. I never noticed this before getting to where I am now and I am glad that I did because if I hadn't then I probably would've made it as far as writing this book to share my stories with you.

Life is like a track race.

Whenever you are running a race it may seem easier to just stop when you realize that you're not in first place but it is always better to get some sort of ranking then to not rank at all. If you can get anything out of what it is that you're trying to accomplish then push until you get whatever it is that you can get. I know sometimes it can feel as if getting results is taking a long time but you never know what's about to come your way. During that track race someone could've been watching you for a college recruitment and you may not even had known it. It would have been better for that scout to see you push through to the end rather than to see you give up when you hadn't even made it far enough yet.

Continue to push forward and always remember that even if it may not feel like it's worth it everything in life is worth a fight.

Chapter 7: P.U.S.H

The following acronym had been mentioned to me during my time of preparing to write this book. Although some of us may not believe in a God or a higher power I say to you, PUSH until something happens. When we think about the game of life it is important to think about the things that keep us going and what motivates us to keep playing. Even when it feels like we may want to give up, we always have to be reminded of why we continued to play in the first place. In this chapter I'd like to just reflect on my own life for a moment to inspire you all to push through even when you feel like there's nothing left.

Four years ago I walked across my high school stage and accepted my diploma with pride being that it was a rough road before getting to that day. To me this is the moment right before it all starts; it is when we choose to either keep playing at life or when we choose to just let whatever happens happen.

I chose to keep playing.

I went on to the next level of the game which was my freshman year of college. During my freshman year I first became a part of the EOF program (equal opportunity funds) which helped me to start the beginning of many new friendships and life lessons. During my time in EOF I gained a boost of confidence as far as my village was concerned and decided that once actual classes had begun in the fall that I would run for the position as the freshman class president.

Well, what do you know?

I became my freshman class president and it became the most life changing situation that I had ever been in. People at that time started to know me before I even knew who they were. I worked with and met a lot of people from around the community and everything had become about people and more people. Eventually, the people thing started to become too much for me.

I shut down.

I ended up falling into a deep depression that cost me the end of my freshman year which I didn't continue and I ended up flunking out of. I share this with you all again to prove yet another point. Now being that college was the next biggest thing after completing high school, I grew embarrassed and ashamed of the fact that I just couldn't finish. I had been through enough within that year to make anyone want to give up. That was the end. I thought my life was over. I was a college dropout and there was no turning back from it once I was gone. My game wasn't over yet in my mind so it was then that I had to keep playing. I kept playing in the game and decided to make a big move (literally). I ended up moving to the state of Maryland where I thought life would be easier being that I was away from what I thought had broken me. After moving to Maryland I began working for Victoria's Secret and Kids Foot Locker. Retail was cool and it helped me to get by but that still was not enough for me. Although I always tended to fall apart emotionally all of the time, mentally and physically I never lost my drive of being a go getter and I never lost the motivation to always be nothing but the best; hence why I am now writing this book to sell to the world.

After realizing that I wanted more, I took an internship position in DC that offered me $900-1200 worth of income every two weeks but guess what? I still was not satisfied with this opportunity that had come my way.

So, I stayed in the game and came up with another plan.

I then decided that I wanted to go back to school, I wanted to finish what it was that I had started 2 years ago (yes time flies) and to try again. Getting my degree in psychology was major and I wanted it to become something that I could cross of my bucket list by the year of 2018. I enrolled into Towson University, got in and then got right back into the school life after taking off two years from the first go round. Long story short, it's now 2018 and I still do not have a psychology degree. I flunked out of Towson University and lost sight of myself yet again. This time I had enough, I was over the school routine and I decided to just settle for a regular nine to five job that could eventually land me a high enough position to become rich someday.

I started waitressing.

Now for those of you that may be a waitress now or that have waitressed before, you know that waitressing can be a real GAME. It is like gambling. You never know what you may get, and some days can be better than others. I had tried this waitressing thing for a little while because I had no choice. I had no choice at this point because I was now four months pregnant with my first child. The game was still going on and I had to keep playing, I was on the verge of bringing a child into this world so there was no way I could not go on. I waitressed up until two weeks before my due date, then I decided I would return back to the job after two months from giving birth. My son came into this world and my mind started doing its shifting thing once again. Waitressing was not it for me, I had to level up.

Back to school I went.

I not only returned to waitressing full time but I also became a full time evening student at Brightwood College of Towson where I began to pursue my certificate of completion and certification as a medical assistant. For the last three years of my life I had spent so much time believing that it was destined for me to become a psychologist or a psychiatrist. I was determined to get my degree in psychology when in reality, all I really did was waste my time, money, and put myself into debt. Besides my son for motivation, I finally decided that I wanted to do something for myself. I wanted to complete something being that I had never finished anything and I wanted to say that I finally did it.

My schooling took me nine months to complete, and not only did I complete that nine month program but I also finished with a 3.8 GPA and as my classes valedictorian. Amazing right? I told myself that it was the end of my game maybe 4 levels prior to even getting to this point, and there I was still playing.

Imagine if I had given up back on those previous levels?

I always wonder what I would've been doing if I had never brought my son into this world. He was the drive that I needed to just GO for it and to go full fletch. I always wanted to do something for myself but that just wasn't enough to push me and to make me be the best that I could be. So my son also known as the game changer was the card that helped me to win this level.

On to the next level I went.

School is now over and at first I had decided that I wanted to jump right back in and start all over with the plan of getting my bachelors in social science so that I could still make it to this "25 and rich" goal that I was trying to accomplish; but the game ended up shifting me into a different direction. I had to throw that card out and pick up the next one to keep my hand in the game. After throwing out my school card, I have now picked up this creative talent of becoming a blogger which can make me rich by NEXT year let alone 3 years from now. I continued to pray until something happened guys.

I PLAYED until something happened.

Everything that had happened to me in this chapter of the book happened so that I could become a testimony. I lived to play the game and the game allowed me to play until something happened because I never gave up. My cards were being dealt and I was smart enough to hold on to what was for me and to let go of what I thought might not have been able to help me in the future. Psychology sounded like the road to go down but it just wasn't where I was meant to be. At least that's what I had thought but actually, it still lives within me.

Every day I work with patients who are participating in studies to see how their minds and bodies react to pain, how their mind reacts to sleep, and how they are living overall day to day. It seems funny to me how I ended up in this position when this entire time I thought that it was over for my psych dreams. Sometimes life has a funny way of working itself out and drifting you back to where it is that you are meant to be. Although I figured that I no longer would be involved with psychology I still somehow managed to make my first real life career relevant to what it was that I used to love to do. So, that all ended up working out for me. I took all of the opportunities that I had been given and continued to move forward. Although life had me running around in circles many times before, I always went with the next option that came my way.

Time has gone by and I still have not found my outlet for where it is that I want to be in life. I have worked really hard to try and get to where it is that I would like to be but it seems as if nothing that I have done can contribute to my goal which is to become financially healthy. Over and over again I would tell myself that something was working and that I was almost there but in reality, I always end up where it was that I started. I tend to rush the process and if I do not see results overnight then it means that it was not meant for me. I give up on whatever it is at that time and then I choose to move on to something else.

Can anyone else say that you too are like this?

When we want something so badly in life it seems hard to even think about the fact that nothing is handed to you. Even when you feel as if a certain amount of time devoted to something should be enough, it is never enough. We have to begin to be more realistic with this thing called life and realize that there's no one in this world who made something happen overnight. Yes it may take days and weeks to start something up but it is all about your consistency with it.

I am a person that is incapable of waiting for something to happen.

Sometimes it feels as if I can never commit to anything because if there aren't any results right away then I shut down and think the worse about the situation. Over the years I have switched my career multiple times because I would tend to get bored and if nothing was changing then I was leaving. Every place that I worked at told me that there was room for growth but I've never managed to stay at a job longer than a year because I was afraid that nothing would ever happen for me. If I thought that a job was a waste of my time I would choose to just leave instead of giving it a chance to even prove itself to me.

I am not a realistic person, therefore I would always think that it was okay to put my emotions first and to leave a place whenever I felt upset. Eventually I realized that this was not the case anymore and that I had to quickly transition into the mindset of an adult. Being unrealistic in today's world can be a downfall because you'll face some of the toughest battles of your life. Even though I assumed that everything would be okay every time that I chose to leave those jobs, I was wrong. I had to commit to something eventually or else I would've fell flat my face. Being an adult has not been easy but it has definitely taught me a lot of lessons. One of the biggest lessons that I've learned so far is to be responsible and to wait your turn.

Have you ever felt like you were over being an adult because you never got anything out of it yet?

Well that's me right now and I know that this is not easy for us but it is something that we have to start practicing together. We must push and both play or pray until something happens. Even when we feel like giving up on the adult life we have to stick to being realistic and realize that we cannot give up. We have to practice the idea behind having patience and waiting for our time to come. Not everyone out there will make it to where it is that they may want to be, but you and I reader we are going all the way. It is time that we grow a sense of understanding about what is happening in our individual lives and to keep going even when it feels like nothing is happening for us.

Some of you may have been at your current jobs for forty plus years and you're saying that nothing will ever change because it's been so long; but realize that you have stayed in the game and played for all of these years. The problem must be that you have not thought about change and you have chosen to just be content with where it is that you are right now. In order to fix the outcome of something that seems to never change you must do something about it yourself. If the job that you have right now seems to not be for you then it is okay to try and find something else even if you feel like you've already devoted so much time. Devoting time to something makes it feel as if you have to stay but the truth of the matter is that you do NOT have to stay.

This scenario goes for life situations, relationships, and your choices.

Start over now by realizing what it is in your life that you have given so much of your time to but have never gotten anything good out of it. Have you tried to P.U.S.H through this situation and still seem to get no results from it? Then that means that it is time for you to try something different. Once you have prayed your way through something or played through it and you seem to still be unhappy, then whatever it is must not be meant for you.

I have a friend that has invested over ten years of her life into a relationship that has done nothing but drained her, tired her out, and forced her to lose sight of who she really was. This friend of mine has always been loyal to those around her and she never tends to give up on anyone especially if she really cares about them. Over the course of time she has chosen to stick to this relationship because she felt as if she needed to be the one to heal the broken heart of the person that she was with.

Now as we all know, we cannot fix someone that doesn't realize that they need to be fixed. Whenever she would try and help her partner through whatever it was that they'd go through the partner would just flip the script on to her and make it seem as if she was the one with the problem. Over time she started to believe everything that her partner would say about her. Whatever she noticed was wrong with him, he'd tell her that the problem was hers and not his. She started to think that she was insecure, that she didn't love herself enough, and that she needed someone in order to survive.

The situation caused my friend to fall into a depression similar to mine and she began to lose herself as time went on. She started to think that no one loved her anymore, that she had lost all of her self-worth. She began to stop taking care of herself mentally and physically because she felt as if no one noticed her anymore anyway. I listened to my friend as she talked sometimes and it worried me because I knew that she was no longer herself deep within. She told me that she didn't want to go out because she was afraid of what her partner would think. She missed important days of many people's lives because her partner made her feel as if she was wrong for wanting to be around those people. Her partner told her that most of them didn't even care about her and that they weren't even her friends. Meanwhile, her partner never missed one of his friend's big bashes or celebrations even though THOSE people were not his friends.

I was worried about my friend because she had been in this situation for so many years. Everything that her partner did to manipulate and to try and break her, he did because she allowed it. She was too weak to even realize that none of it was okay and it was tearing her apart. All I wanted to do was to see my friend get better, I wanted to see the day when she finally let go and so what I did was P.U.S.H until something happened for my friend. I cried for her, I prayed for her, and I even tried my best to change her viewpoint on who her partner was because she obviously was seeing him with her heart instead of her eyes.

The moment that I had been waiting on finally came and I was so overjoyed by the fact that my friend woke up with a different mind one day. She called me to let me know that she was finally moving on and that she found something to keep her busy for a little while. She started over with everything in her life and she even picked up a new hobby that could be the best thing that ever happened for her. I was so happy for my friend and I knew that she would eventually come back around to finding herself again very soon.

If you're reading this and can relate to this story, then it's time we try and get you to come back around too.

Often times we lose ourselves being wrapped up in something that may not even be any good for us. We lose sight of the things that are meant for us and we fall behind on the steps that we must take to complete our journey. Just like my friend, I want you to take the time to find something to distract you from whatever it is that is holding you back.

If you are having a hard time with accepting the fact that this is something negative for you (just like my friend) then it'll be my duty to help you with letting go and moving on. Before you begin to P.U.S.H you have to come to a realization and notice that the problem is there first. Before you can do anything about what's going on you have to acknowledge the fact that it even exist. After figuring out what the problem is, then you must figure out how you can begin to let it go.

Some things can follow us for years before we even realize that its what's holding us back or weighing us down.

No matter how long it has been, there is always a way to reverse what it is that you're holding on to. It may take the same amount of time that it took for you to become content with the situation, but you can always find a way to get out of it even if it takes more time. You must try something different and allow the change to be the first step towards the greater outcome.

Let go of what is hurting you, and prepare to move forward.

If this is something that you really want to do then you must prepare for the amount of change that'll have to come with this experience. The longer the problem has dragged along with you, the harder it'll be to get through but all you have to do is P.U.S.H. Never give up on where it is that you see yourself going, just try and remove this negative attachment before it seems to be too late. Find something to occupy the time that you would spend towards this negativity and shift it in the direction of benefiting your future.

Even if it feels impossible it is possible.

Anything is possible if you just believe that it can happen as long as you are willing to put in the time and effort. Whenever you feel as if the change becomes too much for you just stop and start over again. Always refresh yourself and remember why it is that you're letting go and making this change in the first place. Not everyone can be lucky enough to make this happen, but luck is something that can come along and change your life forever turning it into something new and amazing.

Chapter 8: The Lucky Number Eight

The significance of the number 8 in the bible means "Resurrection and Regeneration." In other words, that means starting a new era and a new order in life. When we start over after finishing a card game this is our chance to try again. In life, every time a new opportunity comes our way it means that we have been given another chance to do something with what has been placed right in front of us. Just like in chapter 7, the significance of the cards in a card game are the same as the opportunities that we are given in life. Although we may not use every opportunity for long, we can still hold it in our hands until we feel as if it is necessary to throw it away.

This is my new era and I am giving life yet another try.

As you go on in life, I want you to remember how it was that you got to where it is that you are now in life. Sometimes we tend to forget about the past experiences that landed us to be where it is that we are now. When you think back on all that you've been through thus far it may help to remember that you've been through enough to make someone else want to give up. Always stay strong and remember that you can always continue to play in the game as time goes on by starting over and playing again as many times as you need to. When a card game ends and if someone is not the winner they may ask their opponent to play again until they know what it feels like to win. Same goes for your life, keep shuffling those cards and opportunities and play until you feel as if you cannot play anymore; or at least until you know what it feels like to be the winner. For a moment I'd like to focus on your new era and what you can take from this story to help you with starting over again.

Begin by focusing on where you are right now.

When looking at where you are right now in life, depict both the good and the bad that has come out of it. Although it may seem like everything is going wrong right now, there has to be something that is keeping you going every day. Make a list. One side filled with the good, and the opposite filled with what you would like to CHANGE. Out of this lesson we will gain a sense of more positivity. On your list remember to include the fact that you have a home, a job, food in your refrigerator, and anything else that most people in life may not be fortunate to have.

Shifting gears a bit, let's talk about the things that we fail to appreciate.

I know that I personally struggle with appreciating the things in life that I have already been given. Sometimes it takes me to see what other people are going through in order for me to realize what it is that I should be thankful for. When we look at the things that we have been given, we may tend to compare it to what other people have. Some people may have a bigger home than yours, more cars in their garage, or anything else that has more value then what you have; but the most important thing is that we too have what they hold but just in a different amount or of different value. We too have a place to call home, a car to get us back and forth to work, and a kitchen that we can cook and prepare meals in. Comparing ourselves to others can be a downfall for us because it can get in the way of our progress as far as getting to where it is that we want to be. In this new era, I want us to try something different.

I want us to begin to focus on the little things in life and to show more appreciation towards what it is that we already have. By doing this, the goal is to become more positive and to feel a better feeling about where we are in life. If we begin to feel better about ourselves it gives us more time to be happy and to drift our energy in a positive direction reaching for more of the items that we want. After we have shifted our minds into an appreciative mode then the bad may not be so bad after all because we will begin to realize that life could be so much worse then what it actually is. Once you have gotten your mind to see the little things in life, then move on to figuring out how you can grow those things into something bigger and better. Although our minds have become appreciative of what we already have, it is okay for us to still want more for both ourselves and those around us.

I know that this is definitely true for me.

I am twenty two years old now (twenty three in a month) and I currently live with my parents and my son. Although I had moved out on my own four years ago, somehow I managed to end up back in my parent's home. Every day I struggle with this because I always told myself that by the time I turned twenty one I'd be living on my own and not under their roof anymore. This is not it for me. Although I came back home for a little while which I appreciate my parents for, I know that I still plan to get my own place soon and very soon.

I drive a 2015 Nissan Sentra and I know this is not my dream car. I see myself driving in a range rover or any other recent high dollar car just because I know that I will soon be rich enough to pick out a car that will never be out of my price range. Right now I make enough money to get me by on my monthly bills but I know this is not it for me. I will continue on in the game of life until I am able to both pay for my bills and to also vacate around the world at the same time. I want more, and I know that I will get more as I continue to play.

Some people may call me lucky, but others may say that I am just blessed. I find myself to be one of those people that tend to carry many gifts within the list of my characteristics. I am a very talented and self-driven individual. I never allow myself to fall short of anything other than success and I always go for what it is that I want. I was chosen to be something big in life, and that is why I am here writing this book to share with you today. Even when my mind tells me to give up I still push forward and without me pushing I wouldn't have been able to make it to where I am in life right now.

I once was afraid, but not anymore.

I used to be afraid of what it felt like to fail and I used to allow this fear to stop me from getting to where it was that I was destined to be. I would always use excuses as to why I couldn't get something done and I wouldn't continue on to not doing them.

Over the course of time I started to realize that all of the decisions I chose to make weren't helping me to become better. I grew stuck and content with how life was going for me and I started to believe that where I was at would be the end and I couldn't continue to play on in the game. Time has passed now and I have started a new era of life, I am beginning to follow the new order of how everything will be set up to get me to where it is that I should've been going every time I decided to give up. I have chosen to take another chance at life but this time in a positive manner with more strength and courage. I feel as if I am lucky enough already to still be alive with all it is that I go through as far as my health is concerned. Even when my mind tells me that I can't, it is my heart that pushes me and tells me to keep going because I can.

I've started living a more positive life now, and I have chosen to let go of everything that I finally notice was no longer for me. Some things hurt to let go of, but I must honestly say my life has changed for the better since I made the choice of letting go. When you feel as if letting something go might be what's best for you then believe what you're saying and actually stick to it. Most of the things that I've tried so hard to let go of I would said that I did, but I never really did it. Now that I did it, I am better than I've ever been. Everything has started to fall right into place for me and I can say that I am doing just fine without the things that are no longer for me.

I refer to myself as lucky because not many people can go on through life fighting and being in the battles that I tend to be up against. Life for me is not easy but I make it look that way in order for me to keep pushing along. When I look back on all of my hard work and all that I have accomplished I can never help but to be overjoyed by my success. Hearing my story now has probably changed your viewpoint on who I am, but it may have helped you to see that I am stronger than anything else in this world. Nothing has stopped me from getting to this point not even the times when I may have thought to give up or even took the action of giving up.

I want you all to feel as lucky as I feel.

My birthday is on 8/8 and I consider the number eight to now be my lucky number. After finding out what the meaning of the number was I then knew that it was meant for me. I knew it was meant for me because just when I discovered this information, I was in the process of transforming into my new resurrection. I now want you all to do the same, to use my lucky number and to start the planning of your new life.

Even with change still being a problem for you, it is time that you make a choice and choose the option that is set for your destiny. Without progress there is no success, and our goal after reading this book is to reach that maximum point in the game and to call on our goal. It is time that you start over and begin to do the things that are best for you. There's no more listening to what other people say may be best for you, only you can know what the best is. Start investing in yourself and use your self-worth as the only excuse for why you're making your own decisions now.

No one has to drive this new era of your life for you, it is you that is now in control of what can happen next. Use the opportunities that you have been given and find your luckiest one. Once you find the luck in succeeding then you are on your way to the top. The choice is up to you for where it is that you'd like to travel next in life but start with right where you are now.

Begin by changing your day to day living and start feeling luckier about what it is that you have been given. Use your talent and your current situation as the plotting point for your story. I want you to take the time to reevaluate the way that you are living to see if it is yourself that may be in the way of your own success.

If you are in your own way, then move around.

This chapter was created and has been implemented in the book so that you can think about yourself for the moment. Finding this chapter is luck for you because I know that you can take what I am giving you and use it in your own life right now. It is the shortest chapter because there is not much for me to say besides, get ready and start up your new resurrection.

Take each day and use it as a tool for where it is that you are about to go. Even if you may feel as if there's no talent that you're good at you can still plan to become the best person that you can be. Being rich financially and being rich mentally and spiritually are two different concepts.

You can choose to be rich financially by working for it, but being rich spiritually and mentally is a concept that requires you to start by working on yourself first. I want you all to get on the level of becoming spiritually and mentally rich because honestly, there's no amount of money in the world that can amount to a happy and free-spirited individual. It's time to be better and to do better right now in this moment.

Chapter 9: Choosing Happiness

Life has a funny way of getting us to believe that where we are now is where we'll be forever. For some of us it may have been years or months, maybe even weeks now that we've invested time in convincing ourselves that where we are is where we will stay. Although this may be true for some, it is definitely not true for all. Sometimes in life we must take risks and decide to reach for the stars because as they say, the sky is the limit. When you choose your happiness over what you're dealing with it makes life seem to be more content then what it really is. Choosing happiness as your go to can make it easier for you to see the good in things rather than spending your time wishing and hoping that you could've done something different.

I have chosen happiness.

When I first began to realize that I was officially becoming an adult, for some reason I assumed that there was a script that must be followed in order for us to succeed in the real world. I looked for jobs that offered me high pays and benefits because I thought every adult needed those. I tried my best to keep up with my resume and to always stay in school because without an extensive amount of information on your resume or a degree you'd never be anything in life. I ate healthy, worked out all of the time, and I even made sure I took my vitamins. All of these things that I had decided to do were based off of some perception that I had gotten from other people that I had previously been around.

It was funny to me how I chose to do all of these things that I didn't really want to do just so that I could survive the life of an adult. Even when I chose jobs that gave me a high pay rate, if I wasn't satisfied with that job I would still stay there just to hold on to the income. If I was too tired to go to the gym to make sure that I stayed in shape, I'd still force myself to get in there because at any minute I could fall off from the shape that I envisioned myself to be in. It was draining and I just wanted to sleep all of the time. When life gives us this image of how we're supposed to live and a script on how we must play our role it can become overwhelming. Yes people expect you to always be at your best and to never give nothing less than that, but what about how we feel as a human being?

Sometimes it may be hard for us to remember that we too have feelings and we should always choose to go for what makes us happy. Spending each day miserable and out of touch with your inner self makes it harder for you to figure out who you truly are. We spend time investing in people, places, and other things that may not even be for us. The reason behind this is because we just assume that it is the right thing to do.

I spent a year of my life devoted to a workplace that tired me out physically, mentally and emotionally at times. I slaved each day to make it to the end because the end result was the most important to me; the final amount of cash that I took home. Every day I'd go into this job and the first thing I'd do was take a deep breath. Not only was I waking up at five or six in the morning to be on time for work by seven, I also had to get to work and open up the place at times. After getting in, there would be a list of things that had to be done before the day had even started. It was my job and my responsibility to make sure that the place was in order before the actual shift started and there was a lot that was expected of me to be done properly, just like the script had said it had to be done.

In the beginning I enjoyed my job so much from my coworkers, to the customers, and even the hours being that I still had the rest of the day ahead of me when I clocked out at three in the afternoon. But I was unhappy. The job that I had was not the job that I wanted. It was a job that was meant for someone who had the energy and the patience to be on your feet all day and to take orders from people who weren't even your boss. It was meant for someone without a life who didn't mind covering other people's shifts and getting blamed for the absence of people that had been fired.

I couldn't take it anymore. The money had eventually become no longer worth it.

Now let's remember, this was a year of my life that I invested into something that couldn't have gotten me to where it was that I actually wanted to be. Even though I assumed that the income would add up and eventually help me to get to where I needed to be, nothing changed. Every week I went home with the same amount of money and struggled the same struggle every month. Even though I was told that there was room for growth, nothing happened and there wasn't anyone around me that had been there longer than me who seemed to be progressing any further then I was.

Being unhappy was no longer an option for me. I ran out of the physical and mental energy to give to this place.

It was time that I moved on and that I chose to go a different route because if I hadn't then I probably would still be miserable and unhappy till this day. Now don't get me wrong, this place has had a huge impact on my life and it is honestly how I got to the career that I am at right now. Even when we feel like something in life may not have been meant for us, we have to look back on the fact of the matter which is that something comes out of everything. From working at this job I have met a lot of people that have had huge impacts on my life. It is there where I met my current supervisor and her wonderful family and it is also where I met my current mentor and life coach.

Both of these women have been a part of the positive changes that are happening in my life. They have both placed me in positions that allow me to be a better me. Here at my job I am meeting some new friends and people that are so positive. There is nothing but great energy in my workplace and everyone tends to bring nothing but good vibes my way. Sometimes it feels like the work day is growing overwhelming and a lot of people in here feel the same way as me. But, we never leave one another in the mood of not wanting to be there. We go for walks, we stop and get food together, and we even take a stroll to each other's offices and just take a breather for a second.

It is amazing and I never thought I'd see the day that a workplace could become so comfortable and free. Even when the work day is packed with patients and studies we still manage to keep in tack with each other and to help each other through the day. Along with helping me through the day is my life coach. My life coach was a former customer of mine at the previous workplace and she was a part of a beautiful family that I adore so much as well.

Both she and her husband were there on my last day of work. I tried my best to cover up what I was experiencing but as always I wear my heart on my sleeve and on this day I wasn't my usual self. I was very quiet and gloomy. The expressions on my face and the tears in my eyes let them both know that I wasn't okay. The family had just brought a new baby into the world and he was at the job on this day as well. My coach knew that I wasn't okay and she allowed me to hold the baby long enough that my heart grew warm and I was coming back around again. Just from holding her baby and from her being there for me on this tough last day, I knew that she would be a continued part of my life forever.

We exchanged Facebook information and just the other day I came across her name in a "Mom to Momprenuer" group that we both were a part of. I reached out to her letting her know all of the great things that I had been up to and little did I know, she was into the same things that I was planning to pursue. I shared all of my great ideas with her and she has continuously pushed me to be a better me each day. It is amazing how just from meeting her in that workplace that I dreaded, she became the closest thing to a second mother that I've ever had.

You see how this has played out?

It was meant for me to spend time at the job that made me tired and mentally incapable of going on. I served my time there and in return blessings had begun to flow my way. So listen, I am not telling you to just leave where you are right now and to go on and do whatever makes you happy. I'm not telling you to quit your job today because it's not where you want to be and you just don't care anymore. I am encouraging you all to stay positive and to realize that the greater good comes from something bad. Although you may feel tired and overwhelmed with where you are right now, always remember that better days are coming. Time will continue to go on and you will begin to realize that where you are right now has a purpose and reason behind it. Even when you feel as if you are not where you're supposed to be right now, choose your happiness over your negative thoughts. Find the good in where you are and make the best of it even if it seems to be in the way of where you are trying to go.

Most of us wake up each day and begin the day by complaining or not being happy about where it is that we are headed. Whether if it be to the job that you aren't happy with, the job that is barely paying the bills; whatever it may be turn that negative energy into positive energy and find something to be thankful for every time you enter that space. Stop starting your days with the thoughts of wanting it to "just be over already". Begin your day by being happy about the fact that you're seeing another day and choose to use the time that you are given wisely. Find different strategies to use at work to get the job done. Yes there may be a list just like the one at my job that says it has to be done a certain way, but take some time and figure out how you can make the process enjoyable. If this means putting on your headphones and jamming out to your favorite tunes while typing quotes, then do just that. If it means wearing a pair of pediatric scrubs that make you smile and that your patients might enjoy too, then do that. Take the time to interact with different people in your workplace. Stop spending time with the ladies that gossip about each other and choose to go and talk to the woman who sits by herself most days. That woman just might be the person that you'll need to talk to instead.

In order to be happy we must not be afraid of change or afraid of what else can happen for us. Even when it seems like meeting new people can be awkward or uncomfortable you have to take this chance first before judging it. Some of the people in my life right now used to be weird to me and I never saw myself actually building a relationship with them or getting to know them on a personal level.

One day I met this girl and she came into my life bringing out a side of me that had went missing. She saw what I was going through and fought with me to get back to where it was that I needed to be. A lot of people would say that someone like this can't just appear out of nowhere, but she did. All it took was one very long conversation that we had and it was a forever thing after that moment. She keeps it all the way truthful with me and she never lets me back down from any challenge without a fight. Whenever I start doubting myself or my worth, I can always count on her to send me those motivational messages every morning.

This person has been a realer friend to me than most people I have come across in my lifetime. Some of the people that have judged our friendship or turned their nose up to the fact that I actually hangout with this girl, may not even know her for the real her. These are the people that are still seeing her for who she was years ago and not even realizing that she has grown tremendously.

I appreciate her so much, and I know that she has become a major part of my choice of choosing happiness.

All I did was allow someone to come into my life that I had never given a chance before, and that is what some of us must begin to do. In order to get through that work day or to make it through any day, you must get yourself someone that you can count on to bring you back to your happy place. Focus on what it is that you'd like to feel every day and figure out what you can do to make that feeling appear. Some of you may believe that change isn't simple and that it requires too much from you, so you just settle for what it is that you're already doing. If you feel this way, then that means that you're afraid. You're afraid of what can happen for you next and what can come in to make your life what you really want it to be. I am here to tell you that change is inevitable and if growing is something that you want to do then you must focus on doing different things in life. Having a fear of change can be a road block for you because without change you never get to experience what else may be out there for you.

A change that I had to make within the last few years was going from being a one person team to creating my village in chapter three. When someone struggles with depression it is likely that they prefer to be alone rather than to have friends and this was me. I always felt as if everyone was against me and no one was for me, therefore I spent majority of my time alone. Whenever people would reach out to me about upcoming events or if my family was having a function I would always make up excuses as to why I couldn't go. It wasn't that the people annoyed me, it was just the thought of being around them that made me unhappy. I never wanted to spend time with people unless it was my mom or sometimes not even her. I would find myself locked away in my room if I wasn't at work or school because the world was just something that I didn't want to be a part of.

When I look back on all of the emotions I felt towards people overall, it made me sad and I began to feel bad for myself. No one should ever feel as if they have to be alone all of the time. Having other people around you to talk to, to push you to be better, and to just make you smile is always a good thing. I didn't understand the fact of the matter which was that I shouldn't have turned myself away from everyone. It came to a point where I finally realized that I didn't want to be alone anymore and that I actually felt like I finally needed someone. I decided to do something different this time around.

I chose to make a change.

I got back on social media which is where I relinked with a lot of my friends and I began to show my face a little more often. People started reaching out to me letting me know that they had missed me and hoped that all was well. At first I thought to myself that they were all full of lies because no one ever seemed to check for me, but I just tried my best to turn that negative thought into a positive. I started attending local functions more back home and I even started going around my family again. Although no one asked or wanted to know where I had been I was happy because I honestly didn't want anyone to know what it was that I had just been through. The change was big for me to go from being alone all the time to being back around people but it has helped me on this journey of becoming a better me.

My village continues to grow each and every day and those around me now bring me nothing but happiness and positivity. I have mended a lot of relationships with family members and friends that I thought would never be fixed. Fixing those have made my life easier because mending broken things in life can take a lot of weight off of your shoulders. I've met new people along the way and I even picked up some old friends that I knew deserved a spot in my life in the first place. It felt good to be back around again, and it still does at this very moment. I am using my change to make a difference in the world because I am back to my old self; interacting with everyone and sharing my stories with them to motivate them to be better than me.

I now need you to think about a change that you can make that might benefit you more than anyone else in the long run.

Think about something that brings you a lot of tension and that causes a lot of negative energy to shift towards you. This something may be your attitude every day, friendships and relationships that you need to mend, or it may even be the need to change your eating habits because you might be tired of feeling bad about yourself. Whatever your something is, let's begin to work on it. Focus on what the problem is, how you can change it, and also what you plan to do about changing it.

Even though we can find all of the answers on "how" it is the "what" that is most important. It is the choices you make about what you're going to do and what your new attitude will consist of. Actions speak louder than words and this is the time where we must focus on our actions before anything else can turn around for the better. I know change will not happen overnight but you can plan to make it happen sooner than later. Use your mind and open your heart to find what it is that you no longer want to feel. Get ready to turn this negative into a positive and to create a change on this journey of becoming a better you.

By choosing to make a change and to try something different you are already becoming a better person. It takes a lot of strength and courage to make the decision to try something new even if it makes you uncomfortable. So let me just say now that I am very proud of you and I will enjoy being here to help you every step of the way with getting to where it is that you want to be. We must continue to focus on the change that we are pursuing and to figure out how we can make it happen smoothly.

Start by acknowledging what it is that you would like to change and write it down.

After writing down this change you should then make subtitles below it letting you know what steps you'll need to take in order to accomplish the transition from the bad to the good. Writing everything out has always been a helpful tool for me because the vision becomes clearer. Whenever I knew that I wanted something different to come out of a challenge in life I would always write it out first before I attacked it. Once you write something down the vision is right in front of you so therefore you have to start taking action next. Never write a possible solution down and choose to never return back to it. Use this new writing tool as a reference to help you with what it is that you're trying to do.

Again, I know the idea of changing what you've been doing can make you feel very uncomfortable but you have to make a decision.

When making a decision you are choosing between wanting more or staying content with where you are already. If you want something to be different for you then you have to be willing to do some things for yourself. Even though you may not feel as if you're confident or capable of making it happen, stay positive and choose your happiness over everything else. Always consider the end result that could possibly come out of the tasks that you're about to take on. Whenever you begin to feel worried or afraid again, just keep in mind the reason behind the new choices that you've decided to turn to.

If the choices that you make turn out to be failures instead of successes never forget that you are now able to say that you tried. Sometimes we can forget that it was us who made most of the things in our lives possible. It was you that got the new position at your job. It was you that completed that thirty day challenge and made sure you did it the right way. Every time that we go for an opportunity in life we have to remember that it can have a positive or a negative outcome. Whenever the outcome turns out negative we tend to shut down and tell ourselves that we shouldn't have done it in the first place, but we are wrong. It is always great to go for what it is that can potentially make you happy even if you're afraid of what can happen if it turns out to be a bad experience. Always remember to take a chance and to use where you are right now to start the transition of choosing your happiness for once.

Chapter 10: Getting Unstuck

J ust like in a card game, when you become stuck and run out of moves to make, you have to pick up from the middle deck of cards and hope that something good comes from it. Whenever you think that you have gotten stuck in life, make a choice to not give up and to find another way out.

My son was born in June of 2017 and in that moment I knew that life was about to change for me drastically. As time went on and I began to realize that I had someone to take care of, I knew that I had to switch up my game plan and to do something different for once. After spending so many years wasting my time investing in my psychology degree, I shifted towards the medical field. A lot of people will say that a young single mother always ends up in scrubs and an RN position which may be true; but at least those mothers are making something out of themselves. I on the other hand went into a program to become a certified medical assistant. This is similar to being a nurse, but it was going to take me in a bit of a different direction.

Becoming an MA was a great stepping stone in my life because the goal for me was to still become rich. Therefore, I took the time to look up how far people were able to go with the title of a medical assistant. After doing much research, I came across the title of a Physician's Assistant which is almost the same equivalence as a nurse practitioner but you just have a limitation as far as working without a doctor's supervision. So here I am now in 2018, graduated as my valedictorian from the program that I enlisted in and now I am on the road of getting my associates in allied health to make it into a PA program by the time my son is seven years old.

I didn't give up. Although the road to become a psychologist had grown very dull for me, I had to do something for my son.

I got unstuck.

When I chose the medical field as my next option it wasn't because every other mother had done it or because I thought it would be easy. Instead, it was because I knew that I had to keep going and if I would've waited until the psych road became clearer, who knows where I would be right now.

The same way I became unstuck you all can too.

Think about some of the decisions you have made in your life and try and figure out which ones were "getting unstuck" decisions. An unstuck decision is a choice that you make when it feels like you have nothing left. When you're focusing on getting unstuck you pay attention to what it is that you need to do instead of what you would like to do. Getting unstuck is the adult decision in us that tells us that we have to keep going and to try something different. In life we sometimes skip past the choices of coming out of the situations that we are in and end up choosing to stay where we're at because we are afraid of change. When you are afraid of change sometimes it can slow you down and stop you from getting to where it is that you may need to actually be. I had no idea what a medical assistant was or what a medical assistant did, but I saw that it was a nine month program that can change both my life and my son's life. Although I was afraid of not knowing anything, there was schooling that had been put in place to teach me what it was that I needed to know. No matter what road you choose to go down in life, there will always be something put in place to teach you what it is that you need to know.

Have you ever been on indeed or craigslist looking for a job, and the requirements turn you to the next page because you're unsure of how to do something? Unless the site says that it is REQUIRED for you to know something, then you need to apply to that job because nine times out of ten they need someone so badly that they'll train you on what it is that is expected of you. Stop being afraid of being turned away by someone. Yes you may receive an email that says "Sorry but we are considering other candidates" but you are just as likely to receive that congratulations email that lets you know that you have been the chosen one.

It all starts with taking a risk.

You made the decision to apply to that nice paying job with full time benefits even though you had no idea how to get the job done. In your mind you knew that there was a chance of failure but you still chose to make a move because it was what you needed and may even be what you had to do. This is where we tend to mess up in this thing called life. We spend so much time settling and not moving forward with different life opportunities and choices. There is so much out there for us to pursue and to take on. Even though some of the jobs may be challenging or something that you have no idea about, but what is a life if you're afraid of failure? Choose to get unstuck. By getting unstuck you are capable of doing anything that you put your mind to in life.

Whenever you feel like something may not turn out well or that an opportunity just doesn't fit your capabilities, take the chance anyway.

I have a friend who has never touched a piece of medical equipment a day in their life before. Even when the thought of applying to a job that required you to assemble medical equipment crossed their mind, they chose to not even think about applying to those positions. This person was a valet at the hospital and thought that this was it for them for the moment. They made good money here and they also spent most of their time on the job with their friends so it helped to keep him content. Time goes by and this friend finds out that they're going to be a parent soon. Emotions run wild through their mind and it was time for them to get unstuck.

Thanks to the position that he held on the valet team, he was able to connect with someone that wanted to help him change his life before his child was brought into this world. Now although my friend was afraid of change, this person decided that they would do anything for their unborn child and applied to that medical equipment assembling job. Time has gone by and my friend has committed to this job for almost two years now. He had no experience, no background of assembling anything before, and somehow he managed to make a change in his life for his child. My friend here got unstuck and took a chance that has landed him not a job; but it has landed him a career to better both him and his son's life.

To my friend, I am very proud of you.

You have to take a chance with things in life because the outcome can be worth so much more than that doubt or fear of failure that you have in the back of your mind. The game of life was created to be challenging and hard because when you think about it not everyone survives. There are only a select few that will be willing to take chances like my friend and also willing to make something better happen for themselves. When practicing the steps of getting unstuck you have to begin with where you are stuck at. If you think that the job you have right now is not enough and you need to switch your gears, then start there. Think about the options that you have to switch to and look into what is available for you.

If I never teach you all anything in life, please always remember to make sure that you have a job in place before you leave the current one that you're at.

Although this thought of getting unstuck may make you excited, you have to move smart and use the cards that you are playing with to make the best decisions. Take your time and figure out what it is that you really want out of the next phase instead of just going for whatever is available.

Practice getting unstuck by taking daily chances with things that you've never taken chances with before. Talk to that person at work that you never saw yourself speaking to before, park in that spot in the parking lot that you assumed someone would ruin your car in, take that walk around the developments parking lot even if you're afraid of running into someone that you don't want to see. Begin to make small changes in your life that can push you towards the goal of getting unstuck in your big life decisions. Whenever you begin to start small and then go big, there is a better chance of a more positive outcome for you. Even if you're afraid of what may come out of something you have to take chances in order to see the final result because without taking a chance you'll never know what can come out of the situation. Always remember to stay strong and to never be afraid of failure.

When your mind begins to shift into the process of thinking that failure is upon you and that there's no chance you'll be able to face it, remember where it is that you're trying to be in life and decide if this is a chance that you must take. During the rest of your life it is time to focus on what you need instead of what it is that you want because the goal is growth. With growth comes a lot of pain, doubt, and let downs that can make you feel as if there is no point in continuing on. But, you must choose to keep going and to focus on the end result at times.

Chapter 11: A Living Testimony

As my book comes to an end I'd like to just bring something to all of your attention. Everything that I am trying to help you all grow through, I have been through it already myself. I have used my own life stories to try and help you with figuring out what it is that you may need help with. Although some of the stories may be relatable for some of you, they may not be relatable for all. Having the opportunity to share my stories with each of you is an inspiration to me because I honestly do not know how I am still here.

Every day of my life is a battle for me from morning to night. I wake up and sometimes I can't even think about getting up and starting my day. All I like to do on most days is sleep and wait for the next day to roll around. I can never find the energy or the motivation to get up and keep going. It is very hard to live a normal life when your mind and body are controlling you. Yes I have control of myself sometimes, but majority of my days are spent living the way that my mind and body tells me to. It gets tiring and I never know how I manage to keep going, but somehow I keep going.

When I was 16 years old I had my first thought of attempting suicide. I was a freshman in high school and you would've thought that life was great for me. I had just made the dance team, I was dating the only person that I ever wanted to date since I knew what dating was, and everything around me was changing for the better. There were new people around me and I enjoyed meeting new people. I was no longer in middle school and it felt good to actually start the phases of becoming an actual young adult. I had it all, but I was still unhappy. There was a place in my high school known as the source and this is where I met my first real counselor. The more I talked with my counselor, the more I started to realize that I was not okay. There were a lot of things in my life at this time that I needed to let go of because I was already fighting a battle without a choice. I was suffering from clinical depression at this time but I didn't know it like I know it now.

One day I decided that I was going to stay home from school because I was too tired to even get out of bed. As I laid in bed on this day, I noticed that my mind was sending me new signals that I never noticed before. It was telling me that I needed to do something about me being alive because, I wasn't supposed to be alive anymore. I had no idea what was happening to me at this point and I began to grow scared of my thoughts because I wanted to live. It was the scariest experience that I've ever had in my entire life. I felt like I couldn't control it, my mind was controlling me and I had to listen to everything that it was saying. It started to become hard for me to breathe and I couldn't even catch my breath. I didn't know what to do, I felt so alone and I just wanted to die like my mind was telling me to. I didn't know how to commit suicide though and I was glad that I didn't because it probably would've been the end of my life right then and there.

In that moment I finally realized that suicide was real.

It's been years since I've had those thoughts in my mind and it got to the point where I had to share it with my family and closest friends because I was too afraid to go through this alone. It was real, my depression was a thing that had the ability to run over me time and time again to the point where I'd give up before I even thought about trying something. It was a sad situation for me being that I'm such an outgoing and well driven person. It hurt me to see myself go through this, but now I am just glad to be able to say that I am still alive to tell my story.

If you are someone that struggles with depression or that struggles with suicidal thoughts I want you to know that you are not alone. I am here to tell my stories in order to help the next person to cope with whatever it is that they might be fighting with every day. There are a lot of people in this world who go through the same thing that I went through when I was sixteen but they tend to not speak about it. It is important for those individuals to know that they must talk about it in order for it to even go away. I am hoping that my book gets into the hands of those individuals because I want them to hear what it is that I have to say.

Even when you feel like the world is crashing down on you and that you cannot continue on any longer, remember that you were brought into this world for a reason and there is a purpose behind why you are here. Every day may be a challenge for you just like me, but each day we end up getting past the thoughts and on to the next day which is another opportunity to fight. Life seems to be challenging when you're suffering from a depressive battle but it is you that is in control of what happens each and every day. You must take back what is yours (your life) and begin to fight off whatever it is that slows you down and stops you from being the best that you can be.

When I was eighteen I had another episode of suicidal thoughts, but this time I was not alone.

One day I was traveling home from a friend's house and I was crossing over a bridge that took me from one town into the next. As I crossed over the bridge my mind shifted from focusing on the road to focusing on my thoughts. My thoughts had become so loud that I couldn't even pay attention to the road. I pulled over to the side and I began to pay attention to what it was that my mind was trying to say to me. I started to hear the thoughts of suicide again and I began to have an anxiety attack right there on the side of that road. I cried and I cried and I had no idea what to do. It wasn't until I realized and remembered that I wasn't alone anymore that I picked up my phone to call my mom.

I called my mom.

After so many years of fighting this battle alone I finally found the courage to go to my mom one day and let her know that this was something I struggled with. Being that my mom knew this already, when I called her in that moment and she heard my cry through the phone she already knew what was happening. My mom talked to me and got me to calm down enough to the point where I was able to get back on that road and make it home safely. My mom wanted to come get me herself, but with her already there to support me I knew that I would be okay. She stayed on the phone with me until I got home and she was still there waiting to console me even though the moment was over.

I need you to tell someone.

If you are a reader of this book and you struggle with suicidal thoughts or severe depression like me, it is time that you tell someone. I have written this book and particularly this chapter for you so that you can even choose me to be your person. I know sometimes it may seem like no one will understand or that they may judge you for what it is that your mind makes you think; but I'm sure there's someone who would prefer for you to talk to them instead of them trying to figure out what it is that you're going through. It is very difficult to come up with the courage to face the fact that you deal with these kind of mental things but understand that it is okay and it is normal.

My mom never was the type to believe in depression or anxiety but after seeing it for herself she started to understand that something was not right with me. I would explain to my mom that this is not your usual sadness or depression that I dealt with, it was something that I had no control over. A normal person that is depressed or sad can tell you why they're depressed or sad. Someone that struggles with clinical depression can never identify why they may feel the way that they feel and that is just something you all must understand.

"Why do you feel this way today Jazz?"

"Why are you sleeping so much and not eating anything?"

"Is there anything that I can do for you?"

Those were all of the questions that my mom would ask and I could never answer them. I had to find the words to describe what it is that I experience even if I believed that she wouldn't understand. Now that I did that, she is one of my people that I turn to whenever I start to get in my depressive state even before the suicidal thoughts come on to me.

This is something that I need you to try, I need you to find the courage to go to someone close to you and let them know what it is that you feel. This person can be a parent, a friend, or even me. The goal is to just make sure that you find and get the help that you need. I never want any of you to get stuck on a bridge the same way that I did but not have someone to turn to like I had my mom to turn to. I want you to be able to call on someone and to let them know that those thoughts are occurring again. Get you a go to person so that you never have to feel alone, because there may be some around that can stop you from ending your life too soon.

If you have read this chapter and seem to find that you cannot relate, take the time to evaluate the people around you. Depression is not written on someone's face and although you may call it a bad day, there are some people out there that call it a bad life. If you have a family member at home or a friend at work that you notice to struggle with being happy often, talk to them and see what's happening. If the person is not very open to talking to you then please send them my way. I have taken the time to create this book and to share my story because I plan to make a difference for someone. This someone may be your child or best friend and you may not even know it.

I have lived to tell my story and I am hoping that it can change someone else's life. I hope that this chapter can get into the hands of someone that may need the encouragement to share their story as well and to get the help that they may need. If you are the person who needed this book, then I need you to start with right where you are. Today may not be a depressive day for you, but we never know what tomorrow has to bring. Take your life situations and what you've experienced lately and use that to start the process of becoming a better you along with continuing to remember that I am here for you, and that you are never alone.

Take the time to actually speak with other people and to either be a listening ear or be the person who everyone may be listening to. I am a living testimony so I know this may not be easy for you but it can honestly change your life. If it weren't for me being strong enough to open up to my mom, that night on the bridge could've been my last day on earth. If I can realize that I don't have to do this alone then I'm sure you can do the same. If you are the person that needs to take the time to listen to someone else right now, then you too can gain the strength and courage to approach someone who may need you in this moment.

Trying to move forward in life with this problem can be very challenging and it can have those that go through it feeling as if they're incapable of being great.

I was sixteen when I started to experience my first real onset of clinical depression. This was my freshman year of high school and I was still a kid. I was very afraid at times and I would shut myself out from the real world. Although those were supposed to be the best years of my life, I went through all four years of high school by myself. I had no friends, I dropped out of any club or activity that I found enjoyable in the beginning and I even missed a great amount of days being that I just didn't want to be at school. One thing that I did continue to do was cheer all the way up until senior day during my senior year. Cheering brought me everything that I had been missing whenever I wasn't at practice or at a game. I had friends when I cheered, I attended events because it was mandatory, and I even smiled a bit more (well I mean I was a cheerleader.) Being that I did continue on with cheering you would think that everything was okay but that was far from the truth.

Even on the days when I smiled and laughed with people I was still dark inside. My mind was still very grey and I couldn't really find the spaces that kept me positive or happy. On the outside it looked to others as if I was okay but in reality, I just wasn't the same anymore. If someone knew the real me at this time, then they'd see that I was different. You would never see me out in public or at the local parties as much anymore because I would tend to lock myself away from the world. I would try and cover up what it was that I was really going through by doing things that still made me feel normal. I had a big graduation party at this time just to make it seem like I was interested in celebrating life. I signed up for courses at a local community college during my last year so that I could feel good about something and to get out of school early each day leading up to graduation. It was hard for me to go on each day, but I made it look as if there was nothing wrong.

There may be someone in your life or you may be the person that is covering up what is really going on with them. Try and find the time to talk to people more often because you never know what someone may be going through. Even those that tend to be the strongest have something going on within themselves that they may not talk about. The goal is to get everyone to be able to start with where they are right now. Starting with where you are right now may sound easy, but for a person like me it may seem as if you're already finished playing.

I continue to start with where I am so that I can always remember where it is that I came from. You will always want your story to be a living testimony, it makes it better if you have something to talk about. If your story started and ended with everything being easy and nothing ever being hard for you then it may not be a good one. Going through the challenges and the rough times can be good for us and we must always remember that whatever we've been through can be worth so much more after we see what is to come. I want you all to challenge yourselves to take opportunities in order for you to face more challenges in life. There's no need to go backwards, all you have to do is go forward and try your best to start with where you are right now.

Chapter 12: Start Where You Are

Usually your typical book would start with where you are but, I am not your typical writer. I'd like to end my book by encouraging you all to start with where you are. When I say to start with where you are it means that I want you to focus on what it is that you have right now. In previous chapters I also encouraged you to look at what it is that you already have in your possession and to figure out what you would like to turn those necessities into. By focusing in on what you already have it means that you are just showing a sense of awareness. Even when we feel as if we may not appreciate something, it is this time now where we should begin to focus more on what we have. Whenever you begin to feel as if something may not be enough for you, try your best to make sure that you do whatever you can to make that something greater. It doesn't matter where you're coming from or where you're headed what's most important is where you are RIGHT NOW.

I used to think that the future was the most important thing to think about and to consider each and every day. Although sometimes my mind would drift back into the past, the future was always where I wanted to end back up at. Every decision or choice that I made I would say that it could possibly benefit in the future. Whenever I'd go to the store and leave out with something that I didn't plan to get in the first place I'd say; "well maybe one day in the future I can use it". My world revolved around what was coming and I never wanted to pay attention to anything else besides the fact of me wanting to know what the future held for me.

I spent months at a time thinking about what was to come up ahead but it was then that I started to realize something. I never took the time to think about what was already right in front of me in that moment. Being that I never took the time to appreciate what I already had I'd always find myself to be unsatisfied and displeased by everything around me. I never appreciated anything in life and all I wanted was MORE.

More money. More friends. More opportunities.

I've tried to recall a time when wanting more and looking to the future wasn't on my mind but it was always those two that I thought about. Even when I wanted to appreciate the fact that I had extensive amount of experience with different careers, I still didn't appreciate those opportunities. If you're a person that always complains about wanting more and you never tend to acknowledge what you already have tune in completely for a moment.

When we spend so much of our time wanting and hoping for more it distracts us from what we have already been given. In life we pay attention to the tabloids and watch as celebrities continue to grow each and every day thinking that it happened overnight or something. Oprah Winfrey was a woman that started out broke. Before she began to broadcast her own show, she was a weather reporter who was barely making it by. It took her years to get in tune with who she really was and then life turned over a new leaf for her and now she's one of the richest people in the world. I'm sure she experienced the blood, sweat, and tears phases of life but one thing for sure is that she never gave up. You are the next Oprah Winfrey and you must start by focusing on the now which will lead up to the future.

Take everything that you've been given and put it into a perspective of seeing how much you appreciate it all. At some point in the beginning of the book I mentioned the fact of how seeing the individuals that lived in Baltimore changed my outlook on life. The people in this city are less fortunate than most of us and they're life may be far more complicated than ours. If you had the ten dollars in your wallet to purchase this book then you're already better off than them. What we have possession of most of them may not. From the cars, to the homes, the food in our fridge, and the clothes on our back. All of that is ours and we must understand that there are people living in this world who aren't as fortunate as us to have this all. Appreciate what it is that you have and realize that you are lucky enough to have it.

Yes we all want more and yes we hope and pray that this is not it for us but, we have to realize that it could be so much worse.

When I was a little girl everyone thought that my family had it all. My step sister and I never went without a new sneaker release and we always ended up on vacation at some point in our life. Everything was great for us. Our parents made sure that we never went without a place to stay, food in our fridge, and clothes on our backs. I enjoyed this life because I never had to want for anything. Whatever I wanted I would always get. Then as the years went on and I grew older I started to realize a change. Everything around us had fallen into pieces and we no longer were able to do everything that it was that we wanted to do. Well, at least I wasn't able to do everything that I wanted to.

It was my turn to be an adult and it was my turn to be responsible for my own money. This is when money started to become a problem for me. I started working at rite aid pharmacy when I was sixteen years old only for minimum wage. To me the money was nice but it just wasn't enough because my parents had made it my responsibility to start taking care of my wants. Although they still provided me with a home and food, whatever it was that I WANTED had to come out of my own expenses. I can tell you one true fact, I never knew how much a pair of Jordan's cost and what they were worth until it had to come out of my own pocket.

THAT $100 or more for every pair started adding up quickly!

Being that I was only working for minimum wage pay, the outcome of me being a sneaker head came to an end fairly quickly. There were other things that I wanted to do and I couldn't do those things and buy the latest Jordan's at the same time. Spending money had become limited for me. I tried my best to hold on to it for as long as I could (a week most of the time) but I just wanted to spend it as soon as I got it.

So who's to blame for the need of more money in my life?

I would say that the person is me.

I'm sure that the same goes for most of you when you can think back on getting that first job and your parents no longer catering to whatever you wanted in life. The goal here was to help you with becoming an adult, but saving that money was much harder than you thought. After experiencing this I started to realize how much I appreciated my parents taking care of me for all of those previous years when I really didn't pay attention to how much they had did for us.

This is the problem.

We never appreciate something until it's gone and we cannot get it back. I ask you all now to just start appreciating what you have already and to drift your mind away from the past and the future. Focus on where you are in life right now and use that as your point of where to turn to. Whenever you decide to think about what you can do to contribute to your future, realize what you have now to use as a tool to help you with what's to come. Live in the present and start there.

Even if you feel as if what you have in life right now isn't enough, still appreciate it all and never allow your mind to shift in a direction that wants you to just focus on the more. Some things that you have may be more or less than what the next person has but just continue to focus on yourself and worry about how you can transform what you have into something greater. The more that you have the more problems that may occur anyway. So to avoid the BIG problems in life begin by examining the problems that you have now and choose the ones that are exciting to you. These will be the problems that you are not afraid to face head on based off of what you're going through and what it is that you have going on in your life right now. By starting where you are, this includes the current problems that you are dealing with as well.

When we think about problems we tend to think of them as something negative. Take the time to realize right now that everybody's got problems. I have problems, you have problems, and your friends even have problems.

Everybody.

No one was born into this world without having a problem, even the riches have their own situations that they may be dealing with. These may be big problems or small problems but what's big to you may be small to the next person. Depicting what problems are big and which ones are small is something that may actually be able to help you with what it is that you're trying to do. In this moment though, I want you to figure out which problems you enjoy the most and which ones excite you.

I know, you're thinking I'm crazy.

This is a test though, a test to try and get you to find the good out of everything that you have going on right now in this presence of life. Problems that excite you are the ones that you're prepared to take on, the ones that make you feel like you can conquer the world. These are the problems that are placed into your life to stop you or to slow you down like a road block, but the creator of the road block forgets that there are plenty of detours around.

To my mothers who have had children before the appropriate age to have a child (whatever age that is) we have had the biggest problem of them all. We conceived a child before we were even capable of taking care of ourselves or before we were even considered an adult. For me this experience has been the most exciting problem that I have ever faced with full force and a sense of pride.

I became a mother at the age of 20. My son was brought into this world two months before my twenty first birthday. When I first discovered that I was pregnant, the problem wasn't exciting. I was devastated by what was about to happen and it wasn't because I was unhappy. My devastation came from the thoughts about what other people were going to think. I spent days and nights crying over what had come of my life and I started to believe that my life was now over. All of the emotions that I felt kept me from feeling what it was that I really wanted to feel which was, excited. I had been growing a child in me for six weeks by the time that I had found out and that made me feel amazing. Some women may not even make it through the first month of their pregnancy but I did and I was doing it without even knowing.

Planning to be a mother at a young age was never something that I thought to be easy, but I knew that I was more than capable of making this happen. Even though people doubted me from time to time and shared their feelings of disappointment and anger with me, I begun to start not caring about what they had to say anymore. The Lord had chosen me for this battle, and I was ready to attack this problem with all the strength and power that I had within me. Throughout my pregnancy I took the time to draw other problems out of the problem and it began to stress me out. I worried about my finances from time to time. I worried about my living situation and the relationship that I was in, but none of those problems were bigger than the one that they stemmed from. I was pregnant at 20 and I was bringing a baby into this world very soon.

I chose this problem to be the one that I worked on first, growing my son and making sure that he and I were both healthy. We are given the choice of choosing what problems to deal with and how we deal with them. Whatever order you have put your problems in from small to large, start with the largest and then work your way down to the smalls just like I had to do. Over the course of time it took me to carry my son and then to bring him into this world (yes a total of 9 months), I realized that the little things that I would stress about had nothing on the problems that I failed to pay attention to.

Sometimes we tend to drift our emotions into the direction of the things that are bothering us the most instead of focusing on what needs to be done or handled. I had to choose to put my emotions to the side and to focus on the excitement behind the problem of figuring out how to stay healthy enough for me and my baby boy. Every other problem had to be taken care of after the fact because they caused me nothing but stress, and half of them weren't even important. I want you reader to take a moment and think about a problem in your life right that brings you excitement when you think about solving it.

For me it was, becoming a mother at a young age. A problem yes, but a challenge was always something that interested me.

In order to make this problem appear in your mind, you have to face reality for a moment. Again we all have problems, some that are more serious than others but this is life. Nothing worth having comes easy so we must face a challenge and show it what we're capable of doing before we decide to just give up and to stress about what it is that we're going through.

Now, rethink the concept and find that inner problem that excites you.

Is it, making a way out of no way? Brining a child into this world when you're told that it's impossible? Working hard every day at your nine to five just to see that paycheck? All of those are examples of exciting problems. It is all about what you have done to overcome those which were supposed to bring you down. If you had a child at 20 and you're now 40 but your child is well put together, pat yourself on the back mama or papa. If you work a nine to five every day to receive that biweekly or weekly pay check, pat yourself on the back because that is a problem that receives a blessing at the end of your time.

Begin to realize that we've all got problems and the only way that we can potentially GROW through those problems are by turning them from negatives into positives. We must appreciate what the problems teach us because they all tend to be lessons in the end. Take some time to write down your problems in order, from the largest to the smallest being that the big ones are most important. Circle the ones that can excite you and make you want to face them rather than the ones that you are afraid of. If you're not afraid to face anything then circle ALL of those problems and begin to knock them out one day at a time.

That is the goal here, to be persistent and to understand that we may not have it all and we may not know everything but each of us are powerful and capable of conquering this game of life one problem at a time. When you begin to forget that you do not know it all, remind yourself of the fact that this is okay.

Day by day we must take the time to figure out what it is that we need to know and how we can figure it out or learn from it. Whenever we start to feel as if we know it all, this shows others that we aren't as smart as we portray ourselves to be. No one in this world has the game of life all figured out, but we can still play in it as if we do. After making many mistakes and bad decisions in my life I still have come to realize that I do not have this thing all figured out.

I've spent a countless amount of days and nights trying to find the answers to something that may have never even been written.

How to become rich overnight.

I wanted to know how I can change my circumstances right now into something better by the time that I woke up. I looked everywhere for the answers to this but until this day, they are still nowhere to be found. If we all had the answers for the way of living and how it can be done easily, there wouldn't be a reason for living anymore. It would be easy for us all and there wouldn't be a game to play. Everyone would be happy and satisfied and the lives that we live each day would make us all content with how this game goes. I know some of you are thinking that you would prefer it this way, but think about how repetitive and how boring it would be if every time we played a card game there was no winner. It would just go on and on and continue to be the same all the time because there was no end to it. No one would have to work for anything and we all would just have the same things in life.

Life is what we make it so therefore not knowing everything can be more of a benefit then a downfall. Without knowing everything there leaves some curiosity in our minds to figure out how to make things happen. Whenever I decide to invest in something the first thing I do is research it and find out more information about it. If we were to go through life without studying or trying to figure out something on our own then we'd all be a mess. Take the time to do some more studying of how the way the game of life is played. Use your resources and turn them into a tool used for playing the right way along with the instructions that may be given to you. We do not know it all and that is why we must read and follow the guidelines in order to make the best out of whatever is to come when our time comes.

First we must let go of our initial ideas and try something different.

With what you have right now figure out what it is that you can do to test and try a different route for getting to where it is that you may want to be. Although you may believe that what you have right now is not enough, turn those negative thoughts into positives and try your best to see the good and the use that you can get out of everything that you have already. Start this trend by first doing your best to pay attention to what it is that you're investing your time in. My first go around of trying to become rich was by spending time in and out of schools in order to make it to the final days of being wealthy. I have now invested $40,000 in a future that I am no longer interested in. I used up almost all of my time spending it in classrooms that didn't interest me and I gave away days that could've went towards what it is that I am doing now.

Being in the medical field compared to being the next psychologist really has showed me a big difference. The program that I completed was done in a 9 month period and only had me to invest $15,000 in it, maybe even less. But, I chose to spend the first four years of my adult life thinking that I needed a degree from Towson University or the next D1 School in order for me to be successful. In return for wasting my time I now have to work hard again to pay off the debt that has an impact on my credit score which is needed to be an adult now.

SO OVERWHELMING!

I didn't give up after letting go of my first initial plan though, I continued to take the time to invest in myself until I came across something that I knew would be life changing for me. At the moment I've been torn between starting school up again (another $20,000) and spending my time writing this book and keeping up with my blogging site to stay in touch with my viewers. Obviously, we see what decision I have made and it just may have been the smartest move that I made thus far in my card game of life. I've influenced so many people and I've help them to even look at life from many different perspectives that can help them with bettering themselves. I am writing this book for you so that you can also become a believer in change and to choose a different path even if you're afraid of letting go of what it was that you wanted to do from the beginning.

Take a chance and switch up your mindset just like I chose to do both times. First I let go of the idea that psychology was meant for me and went for (germs and blood) also known as the medical field which was something that I knew nothing about. Then after deciding to do that, I am now here choosing to skip school in order to make a living off of something that I am PASSIONATE ABOUT! This was the ending goal for me and I am right back to where it is that I should be.

LOVING LIFE AND LIVING IT TO THE FULLEST!

The way that I continue to survive in life is by using all of the instructions on the game of positivity and transforming them into exciting problems while doing it all with a positive outlook on everything that has happened for me thus far. I want you to try this with me too. Take everything that you were given in this reading and use them to change yourself into something better. Even if the word CHANGE may cause you to get some goosebumps try it and see what it is that you get from it. Take your life day by day and begin to find the time to invest not only in yourself, but to invest into what it is that you'd like to see come from where you are right now. I want you all to try at becoming a living testimony just like myself. Never allow anything to get in your way of playing your game and never allow your opponent to stop you from getting to where it is that you may need to be. By playing with the cards that you have already been dealt, you are already doing it right. Use what you have and allow it to help with the process of making yourself better then what you are right now.

Please allow yourselves to go as far as you can in this game and continue to fight the great fight of GROWING through whatever it is that you are GOING through.

I am here for you. I am with you.

I want to see you all Play it safe with the cards that you've been dealt.

The End

Dear Reader,

First I'd like to say thank you and congratulations on making it to the end of this book! I truly hope there is something that you've gotten out of this book and that your life begins to change for the better.

For those that may not know, I am also a motivational blogger and I just wanted to share that information with you all as well. Thank you for your support, and I hope to hear from you some time soon. Be sure to leave a review on Amazon where my book is located, and follow my social media platforms listed below for daily motivation.

Love Always,

Jazmiera Janay

Website: www.theinnovativeblogger.com
Instagram: @theinnovativeblogger
Facebook: The Innovative Blogger
Facebook Group: Affordable Healing Inc.

Made in the USA
Middletown, DE
05 September 2019